Measurement and Analysis of Behavioral Techniques

The Charles E. Merrill Series on
Behavioral Techniques
in the Classroom

Thomas M. Stephens,
Consulting Editor

Measurement and Analysis of Behavioral Techniques

JOHN O. COOPER

The Ohio State University

CHARLES E. MERRILL PUBLISHING COMPANY

A Bell & Howell Company

Columbus, Ohio

104046

Published by
Charles E. Merrill Publishing Company
A Bell & Howell Company
Columbus, Ohio 43216

Library of Congress Catalog Card Number: 73–94053

ISBN: 0–675–08808–9

4 5 6 / 78

Printed in the United States of America

To Bunny, Chris, Sharon, and Greg

Contents

Foreword

The *Merrill Series on Behavioral Techniques for the Classroom* has as its major objective *to improve academic and social instruction.* By using textbooks that focus on systematic applications of behavioral technology in school settings, future practitioners will be better equipped to assist students in at least three ways. Behavioral approaches, when applied by trained personnel, accelerate learning; undesirable responses are decelerated; and learned responses are maintained.

Social and academic skills and attitudes are typically acquired more rapidly through these approaches than when instruction occurs in more conventional ways. The specificity of instructional objectives, the analysis of functioning prior to instruction, the careful application of instructional strategies, and the incentives for responding, all contribute to rapid learning and efficient teaching.

Maladaptive, inappropriate, and incorrect responses are modified and reduced in frequency of occurrences. A combination of deliberate activities by teachers results in a reduction of undesirable responses. Whenever possible, incorrect behavior is not reinforced. Also, conditions are arranged in such ways as to reduce the chances of wrong emissions. And as more time is spent in correct responding, less time is available for undesired behavior.

Behavioral approaches can be effective in helping to maintain past learnings. The functional ways in which learning occurs encourage the use of such learning which contributes to maintenance of responses. Although maintaining behavior has not been demonstrated as well as initial learning through behavioral approaches, the focus on observable responses seemingly facilitates learning and performance across time intervals.

Each text in this series is devoted to a particular aspect of schooling and/or behavioral methodology. In this text tactics and procedures are presented for measuring and analyzing school related behavior.

The author, John Cooper, has made an important contribution to teacher training and, thereby, to improving instruction of children and youth. In this book, you will find specific information for observing, measuring, and analyzing classroom behavior.

In the past, teachers have been prepared to expect others to conduct an evaluation of their students' performances. Even when others performed these services, results were often dysfunctional. By the time evaluations were completed, those same students were often no longer available to the teacher. Consequently, modification in instruction for those particular students often did not occur. The approaches presented in this text enable teachers to conduct the observations, evaluate the results, and immediately modify their instruction when necessary. No longer must teachers wonder if their instruction is effective.

This book will hold your interest. It will give you sound ideas about evaluating instruction in functional ways. And it will inform you. But it cannot change your behavior. For that, you must practice what is contained herein.

Thomas M. Stephens
Consulting Editor

Preface

This text presents tactics for behavioral analysis. Generally the book is addressed to all school personnel (e.g., principals, school psychologists, counselors, therapists). However, it is specifically designed for personnel preparing to become regular classroom teachers and special education teachers.

Measurement and analysis must be keys to successful teachers. The application of laws and principles of behavior in themselves generate no assurance of behavior change. Many programs in education may be employing specific technologies because of fad or custom rather than verified effect. The application of a technology of teaching should be based upon continuous scientific verification at the classroom level by classroom teachers. The purpose of this manuscript is to provide a basic textbook in measurement and analysis for directive teachers and also for seniors and beginning graduate students in education and psychology.

Even though this book is presented as a basic introduction text in measurement and analysis, it was not written to convert teachers to analytic teaching. Others have addressed this topic very well. Therefore, no lengthy introduction statements on the importance of measurement and analysis are presented. Discussions throughout this text are devoted solely to measurement and analysis in classrooms.

The topic of measurement and analysis is covered in three parts. Part one outlines measurement techniques for the directive teacher. Two types of measurement are presented—direct measurement of permanent products and observational recordings. Part two is concerned with graphic presentations for teacher use and how to prepare graphs for publication. Part three presents some basic procedures for analyzing teacher effectiveness.

I wish to acknowledge:

the helpful critiques from Drs. Charles and Cliff Madsen, Florida State University; Larry Tyler, University of Mississippi; Fred Fanning, University of Akron; and Ms. Louise Steele, Cleveland Music School Settlement.

the discussions with Ms. Cathy Carver, Ms. Twila Johnson, and Ms. Helen Jorgenson, Research Associates, Ohio State University.

the many graduate students in Exceptional Children at Ohio State University who read and reacted to the working papers. Too many students have provided feedback to cite each by name. However, Jerry Barnett, Denny Edge, Janet Johnson, and Virginia Lucas deserve special recognition.

Dr. Thomas Stephens, friend, colleague and Chairman. I am grateful for his help and encouragement.

Ms. Autumn Harless, Ms. Joyce Gill, Ms. Karen Henson, and Ms. Kathy Leopoldt for their secretarial services.

Finally, I wish to thank my wife Bunny for her understanding of the "Lost Weekends" and for her support in all phases of the preparation of this book.

JOC

Introduction

A Ph.D. aspirant was once requested to submit to his oral examination committee his views concerning how children would be educated in the year 2000. The student described several innovative approaches to education that he predicted would become common by the year 2000. After the aspirant finished his discourse, an elder member of the examination committee stated that all instructional approaches espoused by the student were employed in his university elementary laboratory school during the 1930s. Why, he asked the student, do we have to wait until the year 2000 for these innovations to become common in educational settings if they were already applied forty years ago? In light of the committee members' remarks, the student concluded that educational practices in the year 2000 would probably differ little from those employed in 1970.

Risley (1969) pointed out a similar observation. "Procedures which we are now using and empirically demonstrating to be effective were used over a century ago, but have been discarded in the interim." Risley supports his statement by comparing

1. Rousseau's hypothetical account of rearing Emile to the work of Hart, Allen, Buell, Harris, and Wolf in 1964 and Wolf, Risley, and Mees in 1964;
2. Itard's procedures for teaching the Wild Boy of Aveyron to the work of Lovaas in 1966 and 1967;
3. Seguin's school procedures for the education of retarded children to that of Sherman in 1965, Baer, Peterson, and Sherman in 1967, and Meyerson, Kerr, and Michael in 1967.

Many other examples in the literature show how procedures for educating children change very little from generation to generation. Of course, we have introduced audio-visual instrumentation, better quality printing, changes in building facilities, and so forth, but the actual instructional interaction between teacher and student probably has changed little since the time of Socrates.

The history of education has not demonstrated a cumulative development in educational approaches. Probably this is a result of basing many educational changes on historical accidents, untested theories, and opinions from influencial individuals. Yet many may ask: Surely some educational change has been based upon sound experimentation and empirical evaluation? Just look at the number of yearly M.A. and Ph.D. theses written in colleges of education that end with the statement: The implications for the classroom teacher are—one, two, three, and four. Has this had no effect on changing our educational endeavors? Or look at the number of journals of education reporting research. Then, with an abundance of research in education, has there not been a cumulative development of instructional approaches? Why have we predominately used historical accidents, untested theories, and opinions as bases for educational change?

To speculate answers to these questions, we must look to the statistical models used in educational measurement and evaluation. The measurement and evaluation tactics used most in education are concerned with groups of students and how one group compares with another or with the relative standing of a student to a particular group. This concern with group analysis is a paradox because a basic tenet of American public education has stressed the importance of the individual student. Yet, most of our measurement and evaluation is designed for groups of students which obscures the unique qualities of the individual and provides the teacher with no relevant instructional information. As Kunzelmann stated, "Useful information to educators is that which demonstrates differences within an individual. Building toward an educational system which is sensitive to individual differences allows for the isolation of environmental influences or instructional opinions which contribute to and thus change classroom performance" (Kunzelmann 1970, p. 17). However, the reader should not infer that group measurement and analysis procedures are not relevant to certain school endeavors. They allow school officials to draw general conclusions, to summarize data in convenient form, to make predictions on how effective a procedure will be for a given group of students, to analyze the effectiveness of educational institutions, and to provide sources of information for public relations. All of the above outcomes are important for administrative decision making, yet they provide no relevant individual instructional information for teachers.

This book is directed to the subject of a technology of teaching individual students. It is not new procedures or approaches to education that are setting the occasion for this development, but rather, tactics of measurement and analysis of individual behavior. Designs for the scientific analysis of individual students have only recently been developed. Mussen, Conger, and Kagen (1963) concurred by stating that we have developed methods for scientifically analyzing group data but have not yet generated tactics for analysis of individual cases.

Specifically, the procedures presented in this book will provide the classroom teacher with tools to answer questions such as the following:

Was I effective in teaching John two-column addition?
Would he have acquired this skill without my intervention?
Could another teaching procedure be more effective?
What materials set the occasion for increased rates of correct student performance?
What effect do different seating arrangements have on academic performance?
Is role playing producing changes in the social behavior of my students?

A description of the text should be helpful to most readers. The emphasis throughout will be upon application of measurement and analysis tactics in classroom situations. First, a description of the tactic is presented. Second, an actual applied example of a classroom application is given. Finally, a discussion of the parameters of application follows the applied example. This mode of organization is used in hopes that information concerning how a measurement or analysis technique is used by teachers will enable the reader to know the purpose of the technique and in what circumstances it should be used. All techniques presented in this book are described with verbal examples and whenever possible with graphic illustrations.

Student evaluation exercises are presented in the body or at the end of each chapter. All evaluation exercises should be answered correctly before progressing further in the text. Suggested applied assignments for practice in using the techniques follow the evaluation exercises. In most cases, the readers' knowledge and skill in using the tactics under discussion will be increased if the applied assignments are attempted. A final applied assignment is made at the end of the book which should set the occasion for the reader to integrate most of the applications that have been presented. To complete this assignment the reader should plan for approximately eight weeks of application.

It should be noted that in several places in chapter 2 the reader is referred to the appendix. This appendix contains a description of instrumentation used in observation recording and where the instrumentation can be obtained. The appendix is a crucial part of chapter 2 and should not be slighted.

References

Baer, D. M., R. F. Peterson, and J. A. Sherman. "The Development of Imitation by Reinforcing Behavioral Similarity to a Model." *Journal of the Experimental Analysis of Behavior* 10 (1967): 405–16.

Hart, Betty M., K. Eileen Allen, Joan S. Buell, Florence R. Harris, and M. M. Wolf. "Effects of Social Reinforcement on Operant Crying." *Journal of Experimental Child Psychology* 1 (1964): 145–53.

Itard, Jean-Marc Gaspard. *The Wild Boy of Aveyron.* New York: Appleton-Century-Crofts, 1962.

Kunzelman, H. P. *Precision Teaching.* Special Child Publication, Seattle, 1970.

Lovaas, O. I., J. P. Bererich, B. F. Perloff, and B. Schaeffer. "Acquisition of Imitative Speech by Schizophrenic Children." *Science* 151 (1966): 705–7.

Lovaas, O. I., Lorraine Freitas, Karen Nelson, and Carol Whalen. "The Establishment of Imitation and Its Use for the Development of Complex Behavior in Schizophrenic Children." *Behavior Research and Therapy* 5 (1967): 171–81.

Meyerson, L., Nancy Kerr, J. Michael. "Behavior Modification in Rehabilitation." In S. W. Bijou and D. M. Baer, eds., *Child Development: Readings in Experimental Analysis.* New York: Appleton-Century-Crofts, 1967.

Risley, T. R. *Behavior Modification: An Experimental-Therapeutic Endeavor.* Paper prepared for Banff International conference on Behavior Modification, 1969.

Rousseau, Jean Jacques. *Emile*. London: J. M. Dent and Sons, Ltd., 1948.

Seguin, E. *Traitement Morale, Hygiene et Education des Idiots*. Paris: J. B. Battiere, 1846.

Sherman, J. A. "Use of Reinforcement and Imitation to Reinstate Verbal Behavior in Mute Psychotics." *Journal of Abnormal Psychology* 70 (1965): 155–64.

Wolf, M. M., T. Risley, and H. Mees. "Application of Operant Conditioning Procedures to the Behavior Problems of an Autistic Child." *Behavior Research and Therapy* 1 (1964): 305–12.

Part 1

Measurement

*"Until You've Measured It You Don't Know
What You're Talking About"*

—*Lord Kelvin*

Parents, school officials, and state departments of education are requiring classroom teachers to demonstrate the effectiveness of their instruction. In order for teachers to be accountable, it is necessary for them to possess evaluation skills. Evaluation is based on measurement which is the way to determine student growth. The following case about Miss Lucas and Gary illustrates one way measurement can be used in the classroom.

When Gary entered first grade, his teacher, Miss Lucas, observed that his class assignments were highly accurate but almost always incomplete or late. His peers apparently had no problem in meeting most task requirements on time. Miss Lucas recognized that completing classroom work on time was very important for Gary's future academic success. Therefore, Miss Lucas wanted an objective quantitative record of the number of assignments completed on time, since subjective impressions of student work may not be accurate. She knew that without reliable measurement she might subjectively feel that Gary had improved, even though his performance remained unchanged. So Miss Lucas began daily data collection by tallying the number of assignments made and the number of assignments Gary completed on time. At the end of one week of measurement, objective statements concerning Gary's work could be made. Miss Lucas gave twenty assignments, out of which Gary completed eleven on time. His performance was not as bad as Miss Lucas anticipated, but it was obviously a problem behavior. With this baseline information, Miss Lucas planned an educational strategy to help Gary complete his class assignments on time and had data to make objective comparisons concerning Gary's improvement during the year.

By measuring specific student performance at certain points in time, we can determine which academic and social responses have been learned and those behaviors which still need to be learned. Also, through measurement tactics it is possible to analyze the effectiveness of our teaching. Two ways of measuring student performances are (1) obtaining and examining permanent products and (2) observational recording.

In chapter 1, direct measurement of permanent products is presented. This chapter includes a discussion of measuring behavior with frequency of response, rate of response, and percentage of response.

Chapter 2 consists of tactics for observational recording. Five methods are discussed: continuous recording, event recording, duration recording, interval recording, and time sampling.

1

Direct Measurement
of
Permanent Products

Direct measurement of permanent products is perhaps the most common measurement tactic used by classroom teachers today. Teachers have had a long history of using this method of measurement. When teachers grade a written examination, or written responses in a workbook, they are using procedures for measuring permanent products. These types of behaviors result in products that can be measured following student responses. Other examples of permanent products include written arithmetic computation, written spelling words, written alphabet letters, colorings, building puzzles, stringing beads, and stacking blocks. Figure 1–1 presents a classroom example of a permanent product. The permanent products in figure 1–1 are the written responses to computational problems.

Teachers usually translate permanent products to numerical terms of (1) frequency of occurrence (John worked six of his problems correctly), (2) rate of occurrence (John read 100 words per minute), or (3) percentage of occurrence (John worked 90% of his problems correctly).

Mixed Addition and Subtraction Combinations.

Add:

9	6	4	5	6	9	5	8
4	9	6	3	5	5	7	5
31	*51*	*10*	*8*	*11*	*41*	*12*	*31*

7	8	9	3	9	5	3	7
4	6	3	7	7	9	6	9
11	*41*	*12*	*10*	*61*	*41*	*9*	*61*

3	3	5	5	6	4	8	7
9	4	6	8	2	9	9	6
12	*7*	*11*	*31*	*8*	*31*	*71*	*31*

6	6	9	7	3	9	7	5
3	8	8	8	5	6	6	7
9	*41*	*71*	*51*	*8*	*51*	*31*	*12*

Subtract:

13	9	13	5	14	12	8	11
4	8	8	4	7	8	1	5
			1			*7*	

9	14	6	15	3	12	11	14
9	5	4	7	1	4	4	8
0		*2*		*2*			

14	10	5	0	10	17	7	4
9	9	1	0	5	8	3	1
	1	*4*	*0*	*5*		*4*	*3*

13	2	6	7	9	7	2	10
9	0	6	0	6	1	2	1
2	*0*	*7*	*2*	*6*	*0*		*9*

Name _Jack_ Date _May 27_ Score _____

Begin
Lesson

End
Lesson

FIGURE 1–1. *Classroom Example of a Permanent Product*

Most teachers and prospective teachers are familiar with frequency, rate, and percentage measures. Yet, many times teachers may not use those measures to the best instructional advantages. Chapter 1 is directed toward:

1. how to use frequency, rate, and percentage measures in classroom situations; and
2. which parameters should be used in selecting a measurement tactic for permanent products.

Frequency of Response

Frequency of response is defined as the number of times a specific behavior occurs in a unit of time—a tally. Responses are tallied, or counted, when the behavior is readily observable and when it is discrete; that is, when it can be separated from other responses.

Applied Example

McKenzie et al. (1970) employed frequency counts to measure correct addition problems in a first-grade class. Each school day, twenty students were assigned worksheets containing fifty addition problems of two single digits. The same fifty problems were used daily. A bell timer was set for two minutes for each work session. Children were instructed to begin computation on cue and to stop at the sound of the bell. Figure 1-2 shows one student's frequency of correct responses during eight days of baseline. Note that during baseline the frequency of correct addition responses ranged from eighteen to thirty-two.

Parameters

The McKenzie study provides an excellent example of the appropriate use of frequency measures. The number of addition problems was always fifty per day (opportunity for response). Time was constant at two minutes per session. With these two variables controlled, the teacher could compare student performance over time (e.g. sessions, days, weeks). For example, the frequency of the student's correct addition responses (figure 1-2) was approximately 18, 18, 31, 29, 29, 30, 32 and 27 for eight days, consecutively. These data demonstrated no improvement in addition skills during the last seven days. However, these same data could represent completely different results if time and opportunity for response had not been held constant.

Frequency of occurrence should be used as a measure of behavior

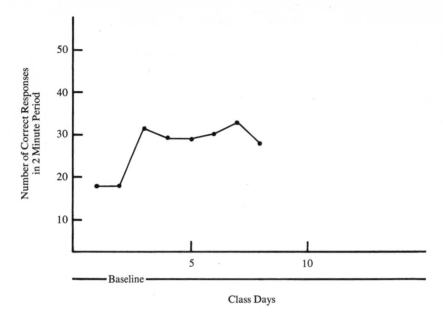

FIGURE 1–2. Frequencies of Correct Addition Responses During Daily 2-Minute Periods (McKenzie et al. 1970)

only when *opportunity for response* and *time* are constant. If frequency measures are utilized without reference to opportunity for response and time variables, student performance is left to subjective interpretation. The problem of using frequency measures without controlling opportunity for response and time is illustrated in the following case study.

Miss Johnson was a teacher of primary-aged learning disability children. John, one of her students, tended to reverse the letters *b, d, p,* and *q*. Miss Johnson was interested in knowing if her instruction was improving John's reversal problem. Therefore, on Monday, Wednesday, and Friday of each week she made frequency counts of the number of reversed *d, b, p,* or *q* letters occurring on John's written assignments. At the end of three weeks, Miss Johnson had recorded the occurrences of reversals shown in table 1–1.

From the data of table 1–1, could Miss Johnson conclude that John's reversal problem had improved? He obviously was emitting fewer reversed *d, b, p,* and *q* letters during each consecutive week. However, from the recorded data, she could not know if the problem behavior had improved because she did not take into consideration John's opportunities to make *b, d, p,* or *q* letters. For example, on Monday, week one, John emitted twenty reversals. Yet, he may have responded one

TABLE 1–1. Occurrences of Reversals

Number of reversals

Days	Weeks		
	1	2	3
Monday	**15**	9	5
Wednesday	20	2	7
Friday	9	10	6
TOTAL	44	21	18

hundred times to *b, d, p,* and *q*. Conversely, on Wednesday, week two, John made only two reversed letters. Perhaps there were only three possible occurrences for reversals. Were the two reversals in week two an improvement over the twenty reversals in week one? We will return to this question, and see Miss Johnson's answer, at the end of the following section, Rate of Response.

Rate of Response

Rate of response is defined as the frequency of occurrence during a unit of time. Rate is calculated by dividing the frequency of occurrence by a unit of time (rate $= \dfrac{\text{frequency}}{\text{time}}$) and is usually expressed in responses per minute. Note that frequency is represented by the number of responses while time is the amount of minutes in which all of the reponses occurred.

Applied Example

Hopkins, Schutte, and Garton (1971) reported rate measures for printing and writing responses of fourteen first-grade and ten second-grade students. The first-grade students copied printed assignments that were typically composed of phonetic drills of descriptions or current events. These first-grade assignments averaged 194 letters. Second-grade children used cursive writing to copy excerpts from stories or poems such as *Hiawatha*. The average length of the second-grade assignments was 259 letters.

To derive rate of occurrence, Hopkins et al. (1971) used time measures of duration and frequency of occurrence. Duration was defined as the elapsed time from the teacher's instruction to begin copying the assignment until the student brought his paper to her desk. Frequency was the actual number of letters printed or written by the students.

Figure 1–3 presents mean baseline rates of occurrence of printed letters per minute by first-grade children. Note in this figure that the first-grade children printed, on the average, approximately six letters per minute.

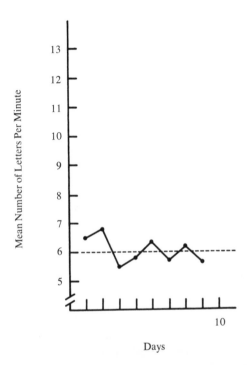

Days

FIGURE 1–3.   *The Mean Number of Letters Printed per Minute by First-Grade Children . . . Each Data Point Represents the Mean, Averaged Over All Children for That Day. The Horizontal Dashed Lines Are the Means of the Daily Means Averaged Over All Days (Hopkins, Schutte, and Garton, 1971)*

Figure 1–4 gives the mean baseline rates of occurrence of printed letters per minute by second-grade children. In figure 1–4, the second-grade children printed, on the average, approximately seven letters.

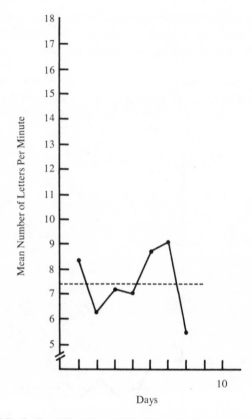

FIGURE 1–4.   *The Mean Number of Letters Written per*
Minute by Second-Grade Children. Each
Data Point Represents the Mean, Averaged
Over All Children for That Day (Adapted
from Hopkins et al., 1971)

Parameters

Rate of occurrence is considered the basic datum of a science of education (Skinner 1966, pp. 15–16). Rate is a preferred measure when
using permanent products, such as written material. The amount of
teacher time spent in monitoring rate measures is difficult for classroom
teachers. One way to reduce monitoring time is to have students time
their own behavior by asking them to note the time they begin and end
a particular task. Instructions for recording may be printed on assigned
material or given verbally. For example: Time started—10:00; Time
stopped—10:25; Total time—25. The teacher or students can calculate

rate of response. Occasionally, students will not have acquired skills in "telling time." When this occurs the teacher could draw two clocks without time hands on the students' materials. (Some teachers have a rubber stamp of a clock face without time hands for this purpose.) Students could then be taught to copy the position of the big and little hands on the classroom clock when they start and stop. For example:

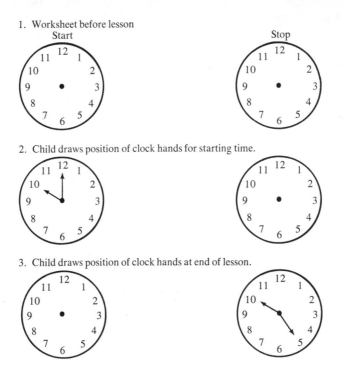

1. Worksheet before lesson
   Start   Stop

2. Child draws position of clock hands for starting time.

3. Child draws position of clock hands at end of lesson.

The relationship between correct and error rate generates the same type of information as is obtained with percentage (to be discussed later) and frequency measures. Additionally, rate measures are sensitive to proficiency of student performances because Kunzelmann (1970, p. 31) states that "the student who worked 10 minutes and got 80 problems correct with a correct rate of 8 problems per minute on the 100-item test is much more proficient than the student who took 20 minutes, also 80 problems correct, but who had a correct rate of 4 problems a minute." This statement must assume similar difficulty or the same problems. Basically, then, rate is important for meaningful data concerning level of student performance. Finally, of all measures of permanent products, rate is most sensitive to the effects of teaching tactics on student responses because it will show very small increments of behavior change.

Remember, Miss Johnson asked the question, "Were the two letter reversals in week two an improvement over the twenty reversals in week one?" Miss Johnson cannot answer this question because time and opportunity for response were not recorded. Let's suppose that Miss Johnson took into consideration: (1) the opportunity for writing letters b, d, p, and q; (2) the amount of time John spent on the written assignment, and (3) the number of nonreversed b, d, p, and q letters as well as the reversed letters. With these three types of information, Miss Johnson can easily demonstrate whether John's reversal problem did or did not change.

Concerning opportunity for response, John's written assignment was comparable in number of words on the nine measurement days reported earlier. The smallest number of b, d, p, and q letters occurring in the assignments was thirty and a maximum of forty-one. The nine-day average number of b, d, p, and q letters was thirty-three. Therefore, there was only a small variance in the opportunity for John to write his letters. At no time did he reach the limit on opportunity for response. John's reversed and nonreversed letters and time worked on the assignment are presented in table 1–2.

TABLE 1–2. Reversed and Nonreversed Letters

Time and Number of b, d, p, and q Letters

Days	Reversed	Nonreversed	Time
		Week 1	
Monday	15	2	3 min.
Wednesday	20	1	5 min.
Friday	9	1	2 min.
		Week 2	
Monday	9	5	2 min.
Wednesday	2	9	2 min.
Friday	10	15	5 min.
		Week 3	
Monday	5	15	5 min.
Wednesday	7	20	6 min.
Friday	6	23	4 min.

Miss Johnson converted John's frequency of letter writing to rate of letter writing per minute since the amount of time that John worked on his assignment varied from day to day. Miss Johnson was correct in converting to rate of response. If she had not, a day by day comparison of John's letter responses could not be made. This would be analogous to the high school English teacher who said that last month Bill read at a rate of 250 words per minute but this month he is up to a rate of 400 words per minute. We could not compare Bill's reading performance if the teacher had not converted words read to words read per unit of time.

Miss Johnson converted to rate of response by dividing the frequency of response by time. For example on Monday, week one, John reversed fifteen letters in three minutes. This is a rate of 5.0 reversed letters per minute ($15/3 = 5$). John's nonreversed *d, b, p,* and *q* letters on Monday, week one, were two. This is a rate of 0.7 nonreversed letters per minute ($2/3 = 0.67 = 0.7$). John's rate per minute of reversed and nonreversed *b, d, p,* and *q* letters is shown in table 1–3.

Table 1–3. Rate of Reversed and Nonreversed Letters

		Reversed	Nonreversed
	Monday	5.0	0.7*
Week 1	Tuesday	4.0	0.2*
	Wednesday	5.0	0.5
	Monday	5.0	3.0
Week 2	Tuesday	1.0	5.0
	Wednesday	2.0	3.0
	Monday	1.0	3.0
Week 3	Tuesday	1.0	3.0
	Wednesday	2.0	6.0

*Note: The rate of 0.7 (seven-tenths of a response per minute) could be read as 7 nonreversed responses in 10 minutes. Similarly a rate of 0.2 (two-tenths of a response per minute) would be the same as 2 responses in 10 minutes.

Miss Johnson can now state with some assurance that John's reversal problem is improving. The rate of nonreversed *b, d, p,* and *q* letters is accelerating and the rate of reversed letters is decelerating in occurrence.

Percentage of Response

Percentage of response is a ratio that reports data as a given amount in every hundred responses. Percentage is usually obtained by dividing the total opportunities for response (e.g. 25 test items) into the number of correct or incorrect responses (17 correct answers) and multiplying that result by 100 ($17/25 = .68 \times 100 = 68\%$).

Applied Example

Hopkins et al. (1971) were concerned with the relationships between correct and incorrect letter responses. Each student's letter responses were scored by drawing circles around incorrect responses. Criteria for incorrect responses were as follows (Hopkins et al. 1971):

1) All omissions of assigned letters
2) Substitutions of letters in place of those assigned
3) Reversals, e.g., printing or writing ⟩⟨ instead of K
4) Omitting any part of a letter, e.g., failing to cross a t
5) A failure of any vertical stroke to be within 15 degrees of the perpendicular to the base line (printing) or failure of written letters to be consistently slanted about 60 degrees from the baseline
6) Short lower case letters being less than half as tall as the distance between the baseline and the center line or being more than 50% taller than the distance between the baseline and the center line
7) Tall lower case or upper case letters being less than 75% as tall as the distance between the baseline and top line or being more than 25% taller than this distance
8) Lower case letters, which should extend below the base line, e.g., y, failing to extend below the base line at least 50% of the distance between the base and center lines or extending further than 100% of this distance

Total number of errors were tallied and written at the top of each student's copy paper.

Hopkins et al. reported the mean proportion of errors per letter each day. This was computed by dividing the total number of errors by the total number of letter responses. Percentage was then obtained by multiplying the quotient by 100. Figures 1–5 and 1–6 show the percentage of errors per letter during baseline for the first and second grades.

Parameters

Ideally, if the divisor is less than 100, percentages should not be computed (Guilford 1965, p. 16). In the Hopkins et al. (1971) study, the divisor for the first-grade class averaged 194 letter responses, with an average of 259 responses for the second grade. Guilford (1965, p. 16) states that if a lower limit must be set, it is unwise to compute percentages when the divisor is less than 20. The addition of only one frequency in the numerator will produce a corresponding change of at least 5 percent when the divisor is less than 20. For example, suppose that a student answered 11 questions correctly from a 13-item test, he would

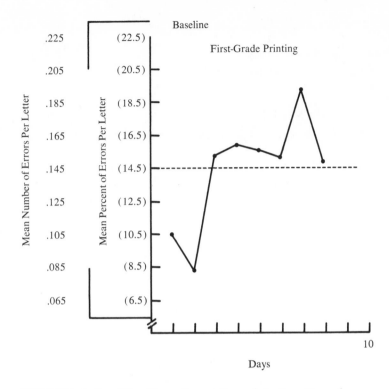

FIGURE 1–5.   *The Mean Proportion of Letters Scored as Errors. Each Data Point Represents the Mean, Averaged Over All Children for That Day. The Horizontal Dashed Lines Are the Means of the Daily Means Averaged Over All Days (Adapted from Hopkins et al. 1971)*

have scored 86 percent correct ($11/13 \times 100 = 86\%$). However, had the student emitted one additional correct answer his percentage would have been 92 percent ($12/13 \times 100 = 92\%$), an increase of 6 percent! When this situation occurs, it is recommended that a ratio of total correct and total opportunities ($12/13$) be used, rather than percentage.

One other caution should be noted in using percentages. Frequently teachers incorrectly report a mean or average percentage that was calculated from other percent scores. For example, suppose Jim's arithmetic test scores were as follows: 72%, 88%, 80%, 100%, and 90%. It would be *incorrect* to figure Jim's average percentage correct score for the five tests with the following procedure.

$$72\%$$
$$88\%$$
$$+\quad 80\%$$
$$100\%$$
$$90\%$$

$$5\ \overline{\ 430\ }$$

$$86\% = \text{an } \textit{incorrect} \text{ average score}$$

To calculate the mean percentage correct for the five tests, we must use frequency scores. If the total possible correct responses for Jim's five tests were 150, and he responded correctly to 132 test items, his mean or average percentage correct would be 88%.

$$\frac{132 = \text{number of correct responses}}{150 = \text{total possible correct}} = 0.88 \times 100 = 88\% \text{ average}$$

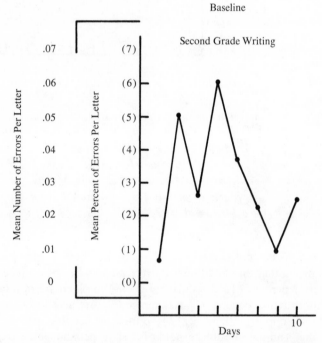

FIGURE 1–6.   *The Mean Proportion of Letters Scored as Errors. Each Data Point Represents the Mean, Averaged Over All Children for That Day (Adapted from Hopkins et al. 1971)*

There are two advantages to using percentages. First, the use of percentages is an efficient way to deal with large numbers of responses and second, most people easily understand percentages. But there are also disadvantages. First, percentages do not show proficiency, i.e. percentage may increase but error rate remains the same or increases. Second, a percentage figure is one additional step removed from the actual behavior.

Evaluation

You may choose to evaluate how well you comprehend measurement of permanent products by responding to the following test items. Cover the answer column with a sheet of paper; then write your answers in the blank spaces provided. The correct answers may then be checked.

written arithmetic computation coloring written spelling words stringing beads	1. List four examples of permanent products. a. b. c. d.
after (subsequent to)	2. Permanent products can be measured _____ the student's behavior.
frequency rate percent	3. Responses that generate permanent products can be translated into numerical terms of _____, _____ or _____.
Frequency	4. _____ refers to the number of times a specific behavior occurred—a tally.
opportunity for response; time	5. Frequency of occurrence should be used as a measure of behavior only when _____ _____ and _____ are constant.
subjective interpretation	6. If frequency measures are utilized without reference to *opportunity for response* and *time* variables, student performance is left to _____ _____.
Rate	7. _____ is defined as the frequency of occurrence during a unit of time.

frequency
time

8. Rate is calculated by dividing the _____ by _____.

$$\frac{\text{frequency}}{\text{time}}$$

9. rate = _____

minute

10. Rate is usually expressed in responses per _____.

rate of occurrence

11. The basic datum of a science of education is _____ _____.

Percentage

12. _____ is a ratio that reports data as a given amount in every hundred responses.

20

13. It is unwise to compute percentages when the divisor is less than _____.

Exercise 1–1

1. In Figure 1–1, what is the frequency of reversed two-digit number sums above ten (e.g. student wrote 21 for 12, etc.)?
2. In Figure 1–1, what is the frequency of nonreversed two-digit number sums above ten?
3. In Figure 1–1, what is the rate per minute of reversed two-digit number sums above ten?
4. In Figure 1–1, what is the rate per minute of nonreversed two-digit number sums above ten?
5. In Figure 1–1, what percentage of two-digit number sums above ten is reversed?

References

Guilford, J. P. *Fundamental Statistics in Psychology and Education.* New York: McGraw-Hill, 1965.

Hopkins, B. L., R. C. Schutte, and K. L. Garton. "Effects of Access to a Playroom on the Rate and Quality of Printing and Writing of First and Second-Grade Students." *Journal of Applied Behavior Analysis* 4 (1971): 77–87.

Kunzelman, H. P. *Precision Teaching.* Special Child Publications, Seattle, 1970.

McKenzie, H. S., A. N. Egner, M. R. Knight, P. F. Perelman, B. M. Schneider, and J. S. Garvin. "Training Consulting Teachers to Assist Elementary Teachers in the Management and Education of Handicapped Children." *Exceptional Children* 37 (1970): 137–43.

Skinner, B. F. "Operant Behavior." In W. K. Honig, ed. *Operant Behavior: Areas of Research and Application.* New York: Appleton-Century-Crofts, 1966, pp. 12–32.

2

Observational
Recording

Chapter 1 was concerned with direct measurement of permanent products. Measurement of permanent products is the foundation for most classroom evaluation. Indeed this measurement tactic should always remain a major source of data for teachers. Yet, as instructional technology develops through behavior analysis, many teachers now see that observational recording is an equally important measurement tactic.

Classroom teachers are concerned with many socially significant behaviors that do not result in permanent products. These behaviors must be observed and recorded as they occur. When teachers look at behavior and produce records of that behavior as it occurs, they are engaging in *observational recording.*

By way of illustration, let us look at a problem behavior in Mr. Clamer's fifth-grade class. Mary Jane has been a source of disruption to Mr. Clamer's class for the past three weeks. Whenever she is called on to participate in class discussions, asked a question, given a directive, or other interaction, she defiantly responds by shaking her head no—much to the amusement of her classmates.

(Question: When Mary Jane shakes her head no, does it leave a permanent product that could be measured one week after it occurred? Answer: Of course not! Observational recording must be used to measure this behavior.)

At first, Mr. Clamer ignored Mary Jane's gestures of "no" hoping that it would cease. But, to the contrary, he decided that this gesture was increasing and planned an intervention tactic. He made a daily tally of the number of occurrences of "no" gestures for five consecutive school days before introducing intervention. With these data, Mr. Clamer could determine whether Mary Jane shook her head "no" less often during intervention than she did before the treatment.

Other examples of socially significant school behaviors that require observational recording include:

> verbal responses to teacher questions
> cooperation
> increases in sentence speaking
> teasing
> guffaw laughing
> aggressive hitting
> noise level in the lunchroom.

Chapter 2 addresses the topic of observational recording. Hall (1971) outlined five major observational recording techniques for teachers: (1) continuous recording, (2) event recording, (3) duration recording, (4) interval recording, and (5) time sampling. Each of these observational recording techniques will be presented and after studying chapter 2 you should be able to:

1. give applied examples of each observational recording technique;
2. discuss how appropriate each technique is for the classroom teacher; and
3. know parameters for selecting tactics of observational recording.

Interobserver Agreement

Mr. Jones taught tenth-grade Spanish. He and Mrs. Roberts, the school psychologist, were concerned with Larry's boredom with school and his lack of enthusiasm for subject-matter acquisition. Their goal was to help Larry develop an appreciation for subject-matter acquisition and more positive feelings toward school. A teaching intervention was introduced. The intervention tactic consisted of a maximum of teacher attention contingent upon improvements in Larry's behavior. Mr. Jones had heard of the effects of social reinforcement and was convinced that this technique would help Larry. Mrs. Roberts felt that social reinforcement would not hurt anything but had reservations concerning effectiveness in this case. During the next two weeks, Mrs. Roberts attended Larry's Spanish class and made notes concerning all behavioral improvements. Also, whenever Mr. Jones observed Larry emitting an appreciation for subject matter or more positive feelings toward school, he tallied the number of occurrences in a daily progress report.

At the end of two weeks the teacher and school psychologist met to discuss Larry's progress. Mr. Jones reported marked improvement. Mrs. Roberts disagreed, stating her observations showed absolutely no change in appreciation for subject matter or more positive feeling toward school. When Mr. Jones and Mrs. Roberts could not agree upon Larry's behavior, they asked the following question: "What exactly did Larry do that caused them to say that he needed to develop an appreciation for subject matter and positive feelings toward school?" Their most obvious concern was the fact that Larry did not complete his assignments. Mr. Jones and Mrs. Roberts decided, therefore, to count the number of assignments Larry completed in one week. When they conferred the second time, Mr. Jones reported that Larry completed twelve of thirteen assignments and Mrs. Roberts recorded thirteen completed assignments. By counting the number of completed assignments, the teacher and psychologist were able to communicate what they had observed.

As the discussion of observational recording progresses, it must be noted that behaviors must be scientifically defined; that is, people must agree upon the occurrence or nonoccurrence of behavior. Therefore, a directive teacher must deal with observable and measurable behaviors. In the case of Larry, it is apparent that, at first, Mr. Jones and Mrs. Roberts did not have an observable and measurable behavior. However, their second behavior definition (number of completed assignments) met criteria for a scientific definition in that they reported close agreement concerning what was observed.

In directive teaching it is necessary to know that the teacher's observations and recordings are reliably reported. A common way to determine reliability of classroom measurement is through simultaneous measurement by independent observers. Hall (1971) defined interobserver agreement as "the degree to which independent observers agree on what they have observed in the same subject during the same observation session."

Interobserver agreement measures are usually reported in percentage of agreement among two or more independent observers. Percentage of agreement is calculated by dividing the number of agreements by the number of agreements plus disagreements and multiplying by 100.

$$\frac{\text{Agreements}}{\text{Agreements} + \text{Disagreements}} \times 100 = \text{Percentage of agreement}$$

To illustrate, Mrs. Smith was interested in decreasing the number of times that Jack talked out in class. She invited Mrs. Anderson, the school principal, to function as an independent observer of Jack's talk-outs. Before class, Mrs. Smith gave the principal a definition of talk-outs and told her to make a tally each time she heard Jack talk out between 9:00 and 9:15 A.M. The definition given to the principal was: "Talking-out is defined as a vocalization, comment or vocal noise initiated by the student. It cannot be in response to the teacher or another peer. Each occurrence will be tallied as one talk-out if they are separated by a breath, time interval or change of topic." At the end of the fifteen-minute observation period, Mrs. Anderson had tallied ten talk-outs. The teacher recorded twelve occurrences. Mrs. Smith calculated the reliability of her data by dividing the number of agreements (ten agreements) by the number of agreements (ten agreements) plus disagreements (two dis-agreements) and multiplying by 100. Mrs. Smith's calculations were:

$$\frac{10}{12} = 0.833 \times 100 = 83\%$$

Mrs. Smith's agreement measure was sufficiently high that she can accept her observation as reliable and proceed with teaching Jack appropriate classroom verbal behavior. As a rule of thumb, agreement measure should be on the average above eighty percent before the teacher continues with instruction. Perhaps the most frequent cause of unsatisfactory agreement measures among observers is a lack of precision in defining behavior. Behaviors must be defined in terms of body movements that result in outcomes that can be seen, heard, felt, smelled, or tasted. That is, defined behaviors should be observable and measurable. If agreement measures are below eighty percent, the observers should discuss why agreement was not reached concerning the occurrence or nonoccurrence of behavior and arrive at a new collective behavior definition. This process should continue until acceptable agreement is reached. However, after acceptable agreement measures have been reached with the original observers, an outside person should be asked to be an observer. Perhaps the original observers only reach agreement between themselves! Asking a third independent person to serve as observer is the best check a teacher can use to tell if she is dealing with public behaviors. For instance, can an outside person tell when Jack is or is not engaging in the behavior that the teacher wants to change?

Some key points to remember are:

1. Other students, other teachers, teacher aides, school secretaries, school psychologists or counselors, consultant teachers, parents, volunteers, and principals can serve as observers for the classroom teacher.

2. Interobserver agreement measures should be made over several sessions prior to and during each phase of instruction.

3. Observers should not be informed of the teacher's instructional strategies. "An observer may tend to err without being aware of doing so, by recording results in the anticipated direction. Thus, if one was aware that a reinforcer was being applied, he might be more likely to record an increase in behavior. If he knew that the reinforcer had been withdrawn, his tendency might be to record a decrease in the behavior" (Sulzer and Mayer 1972, p. 269).

Exercise 2–1

During your next lecture period, or assembly meeting with a speaker, arrange with another person to tally the number of occurrences of some behavior emitted by the lecturer or speaker. You could count one of many behaviors, such as hand gestures, jokes, steps taken, pushing eye glasses up, rubbing head, number of "uhs," etc. Agree upon the behavior to be tallied before the lecture or assembly meeting. Tally the number of times the behavior occurs during the first fifteen minutes of the meeting. Calculate your percentage of agreement. Were your data reliable? If not, what should you do?

Continuous Recording

Continuous recording has been called "anecdotal reports" or "diary records." The aim of this recording technique is to record everything as it occurs. No specific behaviors are pinpointed for observation to the exclusion of other behavioral episodes. This technique produces a written narrative for a specified time period of individual or group behaviors. The conditions or situations under which the behaviors were emitted are also described. The main idea of continuous recording is to produce as complete a description as possible of student behaviors in specified settings.

Wright (1960, pp. 84–85) reported directives for continuous recording.

Begin in reporting each observed sequence with a description of the scene, the actors, and the ongoing action. Report throughout in everyday language. Describe the situation as fully as the behaviors. Thus include "everything the child says and does," but include also "everything said and done to him."

Describe the larger "adaptive actions" of the child, but weave in as well the "hows" of these actions as far as possible. "Nonadaptive aspects of behavior" are important on this account.

Do not substitute interpretations that generalize *about* behavior for descriptions *of* behaviors, but add such interpretations when they point to possibilities of fact that might otherwise be missed. Segregate every interpretation by some such device as indentation or bracketing. Straight reporting must be left to stand out.

Furthermore, Wright (1960, p. 85) offers several possible procedures to be employed in continuous recording.

Notes on the scene of observation, which obviously are needed for sufficiently detailed and accurate description, can be kept in improvised shorthand. These field notes can be enlarged in writing immediately after each observation period, or they can serve then as a base for a dictated narration of the observed behavior sequence. Also, a co-worker can hear this account through and at once question the observer where it is thin or unclear. The original dictation plus the interrogation and the observer's responses can be sound recorded. All of the recorded material can then be copied and revised in an improved running account.

Observations can be timed to permit various measures of duration. Timing of the field notes at intervals of approximately one minute or even thirty seconds has been found practicable. When long records are made, observers can work in rotation; and the time of each observing period can be regulated to minimize effects of fatigue upon ability to see and remember an always fast train of events.

Regardless of the recording instructions or procedures employed, common elements are found in continuous recording techniques.

First, a time sequence should be given. This sequence may be reported as large units of time e.g. 9:00–9:50 A.M. or as multiple time samples, e.g. 9:00–9:05, 9:05–9:10, 9:10–9:15, etc.

Second, target behaviors are unselected, e.g. no specific behavior is pinpointed.

Third, data are narrative descriptions of behaviors. These narrative descriptions should include a three-term contingency of (a) events that occur before a behavior is emitted or antecedent stimuli, (b) the behavior, and (c) the events or stimuli that occur after the emission of specified behavior.

Fourth, the narrative should be plain and easily read.

Applied Example

Bijou, Paterson, and Ault (1968) reported an example of continuous recording with Timmy, a pre-school child. The setting is a play yard.

> Timmy is playing by himself in a sandbox in a play yard in which other children are playing. A teacher stands nearby. Timmy tires of the sandbox and walks over to climb the monkey-bars. Timmy shouts at the teacher, saying, "Mrs. Simpson, watch me." Timmy climbs to the top of the apparatus and shouts again to the teacher, "Look how high I am. I'm higher than anybody." The teacher comments on Timmy's climbing ability with approval. Timmy then climbs down and runs over to a tree, again demanding that the teacher watch him. The teacher, however, ignores Timmy and walks back into the classroom. Disappointed, Timmy walks toward the sandbox instead of climbing the tree. A little girl cries out in pain as she stumbles and scrapes her knee. Timmy ignores her and continues to walk to the sandbox.

This example of continuous recording is written in a style used by reporters for a newspaper or magazine. However, directive teachers require a clear impression of temporal relationships among antecedent stimuli, responses, and consequent stimuli. The four-column form shown in figure 2–1 is helpful in delineating time relationships.

DESCRIPTIVE OBSERVATIONAL INFORMATION FORM
Setting: Observation date:

Student:

Time	Antecedent Events	Child Responses	Consequent Events

FIGURE 2–1

The example of Timmy's play yard behavior was transcribed by Bijou et al. (1968) into a four-column form and each behavioral and stimulus event was consecutively numbered.

Setting: Timmy (T.) is playing alone in a sandbox in a play yard in which there are other children playing. T. is scooping sand into a bucket with shovel, then dumping the sand onto a pile. A teacher, Mrs. Simpson (S.) stands approximately six feet away but does not attend to T.

Time	Antecedent Event	Response	Consequent Social Event
9:14		1. T. throws bucket and shovel into corner of sandbox.	
		2. ... stands up.	
		3. ... walks over to monkey-bars and stops.	
		4. ... turns toward teacher.	
		5. ... says, "Mrs. Simpson, watch me.	
			6. Mrs. S. turns toward T.
	6. Mrs. S. turns toward T.	7. T. climbs to top of apparatus.	
		8. ... looks toward teacher.	
		9. ... says, "Look how high I am. I'm higher than anybody.	
9:16			10. Mrs. S. says, "That's good, Tim. You're getting quite good at that."
	10. Mrs. S. says, "That's good, Tim. You're getting quite good at that."		
		11. T. climbs down.	
		12. ... runs over to tree.	
		13. ... says, "Watch me climb the tree, Mrs. Simpson."	

14. Mrs. S. turns and
    walks toward
    classroom.

14. Mrs. S. turns and walks toward classroom.	15. T. stands, looking toward Mrs. S.	
9:18 16. Girl nearby trips and falls, bumping knee.		
17. Girl cries.	18. T. proceeds to sandbox.	
	19. . . . picks up bucket and shovel.	
	20. . . . resumes play with sand.	

Note that a response event (e.g., 5. . . . says, "Mrs. Simpson, watch me.") may be followed by a consequent social event (e.g., 6. Mrs. S. turns toward Timmy.) which may also be the antecedent event for the next response (e.g., 7. T. climbs to top of apparatus.) Note too, that the . . . form retains the temporal relationships in the narration. Note, finally, that only the child's responses are described. Inferences about feeling, motives, and other presumed internal states are omitted. Even words like "ignores" and "disappointed" do not appear in the table. (Bijou et al. 1968)

Parameters

Directive teachers should employ continuous recordings primarily (1) as an assessment aid in pinpointing specific behaviors that need to be learned, (2) to identify possible environmental conditions that set the occasion for student responses, and (3) to identify possible consequent events that maintain behaviors. Perhaps the major reason for utilizing this technique is that a large range of behaviors can be observed and recorded.

Continuous recording is a measurement procedure seldom employed by classroom teachers. The teacher cannot concurrently give instruction and measure behavior with continuous recording techniques. The recording technique is more appropriate for observers other than the directive teacher, e.g. teacher aides, volunteers, school psychologists, consultant teachers, principals, secretaries, students.

Some have reported that continuous records generate good interobserver agreement measures (see Wright 1960, p. 86 for references). Yet one must question high (80% or better) interobserver agreement measures concerning continuous recording for it is impossible to record "everything" as it occurs in time. For example, tables 2–1 and 2–2 are

TABLE 2-1. Observational Information Regarding
Teacher-Pupil Interaction

Observer #1
Chris, EMR student

Time	Antecedent Events	Child Responses	Consequent Events
10:55–11:05	"Turn pages"—*small group* reading from chart—*Pictures*	Chris turns pages	Students respond with smile
	Teacher gives individual assignments Asks Chris how do you spell		Changes spelling Teacher tells to correct "fine"
		Chris responds correctly	
	Teacher asked questions of Ruby–Glen	Ch.—watches—points to Glenn's book —"That ain't no fire."	Teacher gives him a look
	Chris goes back to looking at his book Teacher asks questions	Chris responds by naming objects	Teacher reflects, answers "fine"
	Teacher asks q.—listens to another child's answers	Chris looks out the window one second —right back—with hand in air to answer.	
	Chris turns page	Ch. responds by doing so	
	Conversation	Ch. offers ideas, looks down then up. Chris talks out about picture.	Teacher asks question about his response.
	Teacher continues questions	Chris responds every time	Teacher says "We'll let Glen answer this one."
	Chris looks around		
	Students have books told to draw O around and things in piggy bank	Quickly draws circle Chris raises hand to tell what he drew O around	

33

TABLE 2–2. *Observational Information Regarding Teacher-Pupil Interaction*

Observer #2
Chris, EMR student

Time	Antecedent Events	Child Responses	Consequent Events
10:55 small reading group—teacher and 3 students (2 boys 1 girl)		Sitting in reading circle waiting for teacher	
	Teacher came to reading— "Let's see your work for yesterday"	He showed paper	"That's good—Let's change those spelling words."
	"What does this spell?"	oh!	"You changed the spelling"
		Changed the spelling	I want to give you an S because you worked hard
	Teacher checking another student	Chris looking at chart	
	Teacher had another boy read	Chris pointed to book "That's not right"	"quiet" (said softly)
		Kept answering questions asked another boy	
		very verbal—answering all questions that teacher asked group occasionally looked out window	
4½ mins.	asked question	held up hand	teacher had another student answer
		eye glances with other boy corrected reading of chart read by other students	No teacher response

34

"Do you have a bank?" (to all 3) asked a question | –yeh– (1st to respond, done quickly) | "Just be still—it will go away"
–no– (then added comments) | | No teacher response
"Oh, a bee" |

Boy reading | Chris grimaces | "We will ask Glen one"
"you forgot one" (correcting the reading) | "Thank you Chris—we are looking at this one"
Started to answer a group question
some extraneous response

Ruby, tell me what is doing here. | Chris answers verbally | "done? Let me see."
"Draw a circle" (in a workbook) | he drew a circle
held up hand
answered questions

11:05

simultaneous observations compiled by two doctoral students trained in observational recording. These records do not generate high inter-observer agreements concerning specific behaviors. Yet, even though they differ in specific temporal sequences, events, and responses, a similar overview is reported by both observers.

Evaluation

At this point, you may choose to evaluate how well you comprehend the information on observational recording by responding to the following test items. Cover the answer column with a sheet of paper: then write your answers in the blank spaces provided. The correct answers may then be checked.

verbal responses to
  teacher
questions
crying
hitting
arriving to class on
  time

1. List four examples of behavior that require observational recording.

   a.

   b.

   c.

   d.

observational recording

2. When teachers look at behavior and produce records of that behavior as it occurs, they are engaging in _____

_____.

continuous recording
event recording
duration recording
interval recording
time sampling

3. List the five major observational recording techniques as delineated by Hall.

   a.

   b.

   c.

   d.

   e.

anecdotal reports

4. Continuous recording has been called
_____ _____ or
diary records.

Continuous recording

5. _____ _____ produces a written narrative for a specified time period of both individual or group behaviors.

a time sequence should
be given
target behaviors are
unselected
data are narrative
descriptions of
behavior
narrative should be
plain and easily read

6. What are the four common elements found in most continuous recording techniques?

a.
b.
c.
d.

assessment aid in
pinpointing behav-
iors for instruction
to identify possible
environmental con-
ditions that set the
occasion for student
responses
to identify possible
consequent events
that maintain
behavior

7. Directive teachers should employ continuous recordings primarily as:

a.
b.
c.

observed
recorded

8. Perhaps the major reason for utilizing continuous recording is that a large range of behaviors can be _____ and

_____.

directive teachers

9. Continuous recording is more appropriate for observers other than _____

_____.

Exercise 2–2

To practice continuous recording, select a television program in which you know the characters, such as a soap opera. Make a four-column form such as the one Bijou used to record Timmy's play yard behavior. For five minutes, continuously record the television program. During your first attempts, the temporal relationships of the actor's behavior may give you some problems. If so, return to Bijou's continuous recording of Timmy and study the record given in newspaper reporting style. Then study Bijou's four-column form. After this, try your own continuous recording again and you should have better results.

Event Recording

Event recording is a tally or frequency count of discrete student behaviors as they occur. Event recording is always expressed in numerical products. Examples of discrete student behaviors appropriate for event recording include number of correct or error student verbal responses, number of times a student engages in teasing episodes, number of times a student is tardy, and so on. Pen and paper are sufficient for making event recordings. However, the following devices and procedures may facilitate making frequency counts:

1. wrist golf-counters
2. hand tally digital counters
3. wrist tally board
4. masking tape attached to wrist
5. tally with buttons or paper clips.

Examples of, descriptions of, and where to purchase these devices are found in the appendix.

Applied Example

Christensen and La Barbera (Hall 1970, p. 57) used event recording to measure talking between two eight-year-old boys. Even though the teacher separated the boys, they still talked to each other during work periods. These talk-outs interfered with the teacher's work and distracted other students. During fifteen-minute work sessions, the number of verbal interactions between the boys was tallied. "Any time either (boy) would speak to the other an interaction would be recorded. Thus, if (one boy) spoke to the (other) and the (other boy) replied, two interactions were recorded. Five or more seconds without any verbalization had to intervene between verbalizations in order to count as a separate interaction if the other of the pair made no reply."

Parameters

Event recording may not be an appropriate measurement tactic (1) when behaviors are occurring at very high rates or (2) when one class of response can occur for extended time periods. Examples of high rate behaviors could include rocking, rapid jerks of the head, hands, or legs, running, tapping objects. Examples of behaviors that occur across time could include thumb sucking or task orientation such as reading or listening. More appropriate measurement tactics for high rate behaviors and behaviors that occur across time include duration recording, interval recording, and time sample recording (to be discussed later).

   It should be noted that task-oriented behaviors occurring across time are usually not a terminal concern of directive teachers. The process of reading or listening is just a first step to more relevant behaviors. Rate of reading and comprehension, not the process of reading, are the important dimensions. Similarly, movements of the student that utilize what he hears, not the act of listening, are salient.

Event recording may be expressed as number or frequency of occurrence if opportunity for response and observation time are constant across sessions. If observation time is not constant, rate of occurrence (rate = frequency/time) is the acceptable datum.

Event recording is the major observational measurement tactic of directive teachers. The advantages for using event recording are: (1) it is easily applied in classroom situations, (2) it does not interfere with ongoing teaching, and (3) it produces a numerical product.

Evaluation

You may choose to evaluate how well you comprehend the additional information on observation recording by responding to the following test items. Cover the answer column with a sheet of paper; then write your answers in the blank spaces provided. The correct answers may then be checked.

Event

1. _____ recording is a cumulative tally or frequency count of discrete events as they occur.

numerical

2. Event recording is always expressed in _____ products.

pen and paper
golf counters
hand tally digital
   counters
wrist tally board
masking tape on wrist

3. List five devices or procedures for facilitating event recording.
   a.
   b.
   c.
   d.
   e.

high rate behaviors
class of responses that
   occur for extended
   time periods

4. Event recording may *not* be an appropriate measurement tactic for:
   a.
   b.

tapping objects

5. Give one example of a possible high rate behavior.
   a.

task orientation such
   as listening

6. Give one example of behaviors that may occur across extended time periods.
   a.

opportunity	7. Event recording may be expressed as number or frequency of occurrence if _____ for response and _____ _____ are constant across sessions.
observation time	
rate	8. If observation time is not constant, _____ is the acceptable datum.

Exercise 2–3

Select a person that you are with for approximately thirty minutes daily. It could be a spouse, parent, friend, or colleague. For five days, thirty minutes daily, tally the number of verbal comments that are initiated, and directed toward you, by the selected person.

Duration Recording

Event recording is perhaps the most common and useful observational measurement tactic for teachers. Yet, some student behaviors do not lend themselves to event recording. Duration recording is an appropriate measurement tactic for behaviors that occur at very high rates (e.g. rocking; rapid jerks of the head, hands, or legs; running; tapping objects; etc.) or when behaviors occur for extended time periods (e.g. task orientation such as reading or listening). Basically when a teacher is concerned with how long a student or class engages in a particular behavior, duration recording should be used. Measures of duration are usually reported as the percentage of time that a behavior or event continues or lasts. For instance, suppose a teacher were interested in how much time John spent on task during a seat work assignment. If John were on task for eighteen minutes during thirty minutes of seat work, the teacher would report that John was on task sixty percent of the time. Most teachers use a stopwatch for recording durations of student behavior. (Examples of, descriptions of, and where to purchase stopwatches are found in the appendix.) As an alternative to the stopwatch, teachers can use a wall clock or wrist watch for duration measures. It should be noted that duration measures obtained with a wall clock or wrist watch will probably be less precise than measures obtained with a stopwatch.

Applied Examples

Krauss (1972) used duration recording during a family intervention study. Duration measures were reported in percent.

BEHAVIOR MEASURED: The mother complained that the subject was not "playing alone" when told to do so. The girl either dawdled choosing toys, persistently attempted to get the mother to join her in play, or called out to her mother for attention. This "playing alone" behavior was to be accelerated.

Since the father was not in the home during play periods, a reliability check was not made.

EXPERIMENTAL PROCEDURES AND RESULTS: During *Baseline* phase, the subject's mean "play alone" behavior for 15 minute periods was 95%; the mother not only wanted this at 100% but desired the periods be lengthened to at least 30 minutes each. *Television and praise:* Beginning with the second week, a bell timer was used to indicate to the child and mother when the 20 minute periods were over. When the child's nap schedule allowed, an afternoon period was recorded in addition to the routine morning period. If the subject played 100% of the period, the television was immediately turned on to a show determined to be rewarding to her (usually "Electric Co."). If the subject did not play to criterion, a penalty was assessed: the child was to sit in front of a blank television for 3 to 15 minutes depending on her play behavior. This was necessary 5 times during the three week intervention phase. The timer was used also to indicate termination of time-out. Mean desired behavior during this phase was 92%; this was depressed by the initial day of intervention and by a second morning when the child's routine was thrown off by sleeping late (past the usual play time). Although the mother found that verbal praise during play was disruptive to the child, she did insure that praise was given when the timer went off. *Praise only:* During this phase, the use of the timer and television were discontinued; this was done partially to discredit the possibility the timer itself was reinforcing play as posited by the mother. Behavior was at 100% for 5 consecutive days of 30-minute periods. Figure (2-2) is a record of the percent of time spent in playing-alone behavior by a four-year-old girl during fifteen, twenty and thirty minute periods. (Krauss 1972)

VanDyke (1972) also employed duration recording during a family intervention study. Duration measures were reported in the amount of time required for a child to complete a task.

BEHAVIOR MEASURED: Two behaviors were measured, both related to drying dishes. The mother reported, and the father agreed, that this behavior literally "drove the whole family up the wall" and disrupted family unity every evening. The first behavior was the duration of time spent in drying the dishes in the

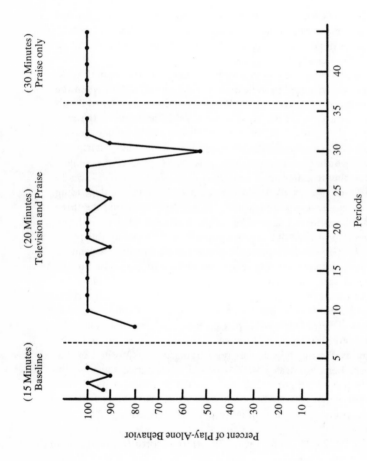

FIGURE 2–2. A Record of the Percent of Time Spent in Playing-Alone Behavior by a Four-year-old Girl During Fifteen, Twenty and Thirty-minute Periods.

evening. The second behavior was the number of reprimands given by the mother during the process. Reliability checks were provided by the oldest brother, in which there was 100 per cent agreement.

INTERVENTION STRATEGY AND RESULTS: A record was kept by the mother for eight consecutive days to establish a baseline. In a conference with the subject, mother, and teacher, it was agreed that the client should receive a checkmark for every evening in which the dishes were dried within forty minutes and in which the number of reprimands did not exceed five. Three contracted rewards were offered from which the subject chose the reward most appealing to her.

(Figures 2-3 and 2-4 demonstrate the results.) It is pointed out that the average time required for drying dishes was slightly less than 52 minutes; the average number of reprimands slightly more than 16 during the baseline period. During the contingency management period of 17 days (subject chose the reward requiring 35 checkmarks and insisted upon it even though it was explained that it would necessitate a longer period of time), the average time was reduced to slightly over 33 minutes; the average number of reprimands was reduced to 5.4. As soon as the contracted reward was received, the average time was 65 minutes and the average number of reprimands was 17 over a period of four days. When the positive reinforcement was resumed, the average time was 37 minutes; the average number of reprimands 3.6 over a period of five days. (Van Dyke 1972)

Parameters

Duration recording may be used in two ways. The first mode is when teachers require data concerning amount of time a student emits behaviors within specified time periods. For example, if a kindergarten teacher were concerned with "isolate" behavior, the teacher could record the duration of "isolate" behavior that occurred during daily thirty-minute free play periods. This type of measurement is reported in percent of time.

$$(\text{e.g., } \% = \frac{\text{duration of “isolate” behavior} = 25 \text{ minutes}}{\text{duration of free play periods} = 30 \text{ minutes}} \times 100 \doteq 83\%.$$

Thus in this hypothetical example, a kindergarten student engaged in "isolate" behavior 83 percent of one free play setting. The Krauss (1972) example meets this criterion. The second mode is when teachers require data concerning amount of time a student takes to complete a

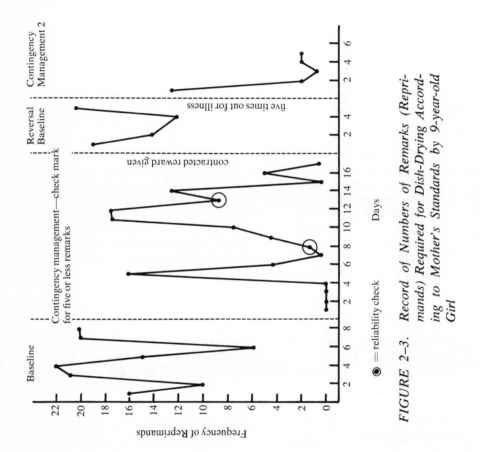

FIGURE 2–3. Record of Numbers of Remarks (Reprimands) Required for Dish-Drying According to Mother's Standards by 9-year-old Girl

44

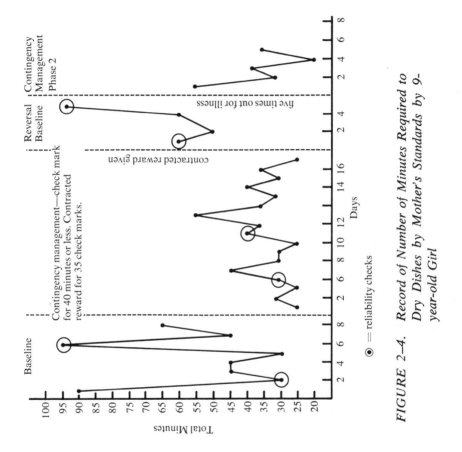

FIGURE 2-4. Record of Number of Minutes Required to Dry Dishes by Mother's Standards by 9-year-old Girl

45

specific task when no minimum or maximum time criteria are specified. For example, if a teacher were concerned with the amount of time a student took to walk from her classroom to the cafeteria for the noon meal, the teacher could report just time durations (e.g. for four successive days the student's time in minutes to the cafeteria = 9, 11, 8, 10). The Van Dyke (1972) example meets this criterion.

Evaluation

You may choose to evaluate how well you comprehend the information on duration recording by responding to the following test items. Cover the answer column with a sheet of paper; then write your answers in the blank spaces provided. The correct answers may then be checked.

Duration recording

1. _____ _____ is used when teachers are concerned with how long a student or class engages in a particular behavior.

percent

2. Measures of duration are usually reported as the _____ of time that a behavior or event continues or lasts.

stopwatch

3. The most precise nonautomated instrument for duration recording is a _____ .

to record the amount of time a student emits behaviors within specified time periods

4. What are the two ways that duration recording is most frequently used?

   a.

to record data concerning amount of time a student takes to complete a specific task when no minimum or maximum time criteria are specified

   b.

Exercise 2–4

Make arrangements to observe a child watching two or more television programs such as "Sesame Street," "Captain Kangaroo," or "Mr. Roger's Neighborhood." With a stopwatch, record the duration of time that the child attends to the programs. Calculate the percentage of attending time for each program. Was there a different duration of attending behavior for the different programs?

Interval Recording

Event and duration recording generate a composite picture of student behavior during one time period. For example, Bill was engaged in nonstudy behavior thirty-five percent of the time. Yet at times it would facilitate educational planning if the teacher had access to temporal patterns of behavioral occurrences. Were Bill's nonstudy behaviors occurring throughout the entire period? Or predominately at the start, or middle, or end of the period? For instance, if Bill's nonstudy behaviors occurred primarily at the start of a study period, the teacher could introduce a plan to decrease the latency between the start of class and the start of Bill's study behavior. Interval recording provides an estimate of student performance across time intervals which does not occur with event and duration recording.

Interval recording is used to measure the occurrence or nonoccurrence of behavior within specified time intervals. The total observation session is delineated into smaller time intervals of equal size. For example, if the total observation session were ten minutes, and the observer were using ten-second interval measurement, the session would be divided into sixty individual ten-second recording units. Selection of an interval size should provide the observer with sufficient time to observe and record behavior reliably. Simultaneous recording of multiple behaviors and respective rates of occurrence jointly influence interval length. However, interval size will usually range from six to thirty seconds depending on behavior to be observed.

To record occurrence or nonoccurrence of behaviors, a paper is ruled into squares to differentiate time intervals, as indicated in figure 2–5. The squares may be positioned either horizontally or vertically. To record,

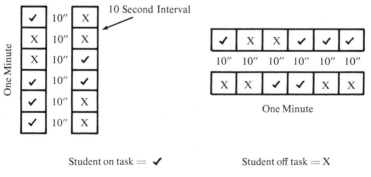

Student on task = ✔　　　　Student off task = X

FIGURE 2–5

the observer checks time intervals in which the behavior occurred or did not occur. Behavior is usually recorded only once per interval and reported as percent of occurrence. Figure 2–5 shows that the student was on task fifty percent of the time (6 intervals on tasks/ 12 total intervals $\times$ 100 = 50%).

If more than one discrete behavior or more than one student is to be observed and recorded, the observer may add additional rows for each behavior or student (figure 2–6). The only criterion concerning the

	10″	10″	10″	10″	10″	10″	10″	10″	10″	10″
On Task										
Verbal Off Task										
Motor Off Task										
Passive Off Task										

FIGURE 2–6

number of discrete behaviors or students that can be measured concurrently is reliability of recording (Mattos 1968).

Reliability of interval measurement will probably decrease when the observer simultaneously records more than three or four response categories. However, the reliability of recording multiple behaviors or students should increase with training and recording experience. When interval recording is used for a group, observers frequently record only one student per interval (e.g. observe and record John, 10″; then Laura, 10″; next Alicia, 10″; etc.) (see figure 2–7).

The interval data sheet for John, Laura, Alicia, Daryl, MaryAnn, and

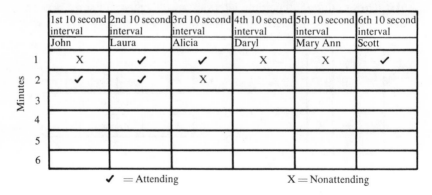

		1st 10 second interval	2nd 10 second interval	3rd 10 second interval	4th 10 second interval	5th 10 second interval	6th 10 second interval
		John	Laura	Alicia	Daryl	Mary Ann	Scott
	1	X	✓	✓	X	X	✓
Minutes	2	✓	✓	X			
	3						
	4						
	5						
	6						

✓ = Attending   X = Nonattending

FIGURE 2–7

Scott shows that John did not attend during the first ten-second interval; Laura attended during the second ten-second interval, etc. It should be noted that the (√) in this example does not mean necessarily that Laura attended throughout the entire ten-second interval; just that attending behavior occurred sometime during that interval.

Another tactic used in interval recording of multiple categories is to observe during the first interval, record during the second interval what was observed in the first interval, observe again in the third interval, record in the fourth, etc. (figure 2–8).

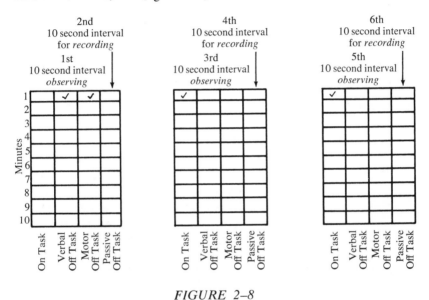

FIGURE 2–8

A common timing device used in interval recording is comprised of *pen, paper, clipboard,* and *stopwatch.* The stopwatch should be attached to the clip of the clipboard. Commercial stopwatch attachment devices for clipboards are available, but the watch can be satisfactorily attached with rubber bands. A disadvantage of using the clipboard-stopwatch timing device is that the observer must periodically break eye contact with his subjects to observe the stopwatch. This may result in a *decrease* in the accuracy of measurement.

Worthy (1968) described a miniature, *portable timing and audible signal-generating device* to be used as a time-base for interval recording. He reports that "this device, which is small enough to fit into a shirt pocket, eliminates the need for the observer to visually monitor a stopwatch, etc. which detracts from his observance and recording of behavior." Worthy's technical note is complete enough so that most TV–

radio repairmen could build the timing device. The appendix contains descriptions of the timing devices.

Jorgenson described a unique timing procedure for interval recording that does not rely upon outside instrumentation. Her procedure is especially appropriate for teachers. She states that teacher-directed presentations (e.g. lectures, activities, songs, etc.) can be timed and presentation cues memorized to differentiate time intervals (Jorgenson 1972). For example, in the song "Twinkle, Twinkle Little Star" (at a slow tempo), ten-second intervals can occur at the words "high" and "wonder" (Jorgenson 1972).

Applied Examples

Jorgenson (1972) used interval recording to measure attending behavior of six trainable retarded children in music activity.

> Attending behavior was defined as sitting in a chair at a desk and looking at the teacher and/or in the direction of the education activity. Once attending behavior was defined, a method of measuring the behavior was determined. Because no observers were available during the activities, a tactic was devised to conduct activities and record behavior without assistance from another person.
>
> Songs and activities were timed and ten second intervals within each song and activity noted. Cues for ten second intervals within each activity were memorized by the therapist. For example, in the song "Twinkle, Twinkle Little Star" (at a slow tempo), ten second intervals occur at the words "high" and "wonder".
>
> Each child was observed for a ten second interval and a check mark (√) was placed under each child's name if he were attending during the ten second period. If he were not attending, an X (X) was placed under his name. Recording continued throughout the sessions, i.e., a mark was placed under a child's name without stopping the activity throughout the thirty times per session. Table 2-3 is a sample observation chart showing the method of recording attending behavior for six children. (Jorgenson 1972)

Hall, Lund and Jackson (1968) used interval recording to measure nonstudy behavior, study behavior, teacher verbalization directed toward a pupil, and teacher proximity to the student (teacher within three feet). Their observational recording sheet and symbol key was constructed as shown in figure 2–9.

Parameters

Interval recording is a measurement procedure seldom employed by classroom teachers when they are instructing students. It is difficult for

TABLE 2–3.   Sample Observation Chart Showing Method
of Recording Attending Behavior for Six
Children*

	John	Laura	Alicia	Daryl	Mary Ann	Scott
1.	X	✓	✓	X	X	✓
2.	✓	✓	X	✓	✓	X
3.	X	✓	✓	X	X	✓
4.						
5.						
6.						

* Each child's name represents 10 seconds

teachers concurrently to give instruction and reliably observe and record
behaviors with interval recording. This tactic requires constant attending
behavior from the observer. Therefore, interval recording is an appropriate technique for ancillary teacher personnel (e.g. consultant teachers,
psychologists, students, teacher aides, etc.) or for the teacher when he
is not interacting with students. An exception to this postulate is exem-
plified in Jorgenson's (1972, see applied example, interval recording)
study in which the teacher both directed the activity and employed interval recording to measure group attending behaviors.

There are two major advantages in using interval recording. First,
interval recording indicates an estimate of both frequency and duration
of behavior. Second, and perhaps most important, interval recording
provides an estimate of student performance across time intervals which
does not occur with event and duration recording. Interval recording
generates information concerning probabilities of when a behavior is
likely to occur or not occur. For example, is it more probable that the
behavior will occur or not occur at the start, middle, or end of an instruction period? These data are valuable to the directive teachers in programming teaching strategies, materials, or schedules of reinforcement.

Evaluation

You may choose to evaluate how well you comprehend the presentation
of interval recording by responding to the following test items. Cover

FIGURE 2-9 — Classroom observation recording chart

seconds
10" 10" 10" 10" 10" 10" … (bracketed span labeled "one minute")

	10"	10"	10"	10"	10"	10"														
(Row 1)	N	N	N	N	S	S	N	S	S	S	S	N	N	N	N	N	N	N	N	N
(Row 2)	T	T					T												T	T
(Row 3)	/	/			/		/													

Row 1 N Non-Study Behavior   S Study Behavior
Row 2 T Teacher verbalization directed toward pupil
Row 3 / Teacher proximity (teacher within three feet)

FIGURE 2-9

the answer column with a sheet of paper; then write your answers in the blank spaces provided. The correct answers may then be checked.

Interval recording

1. _____ _____ is used to measure the occurrence or non-occurrence of behavior within specified time intervals.

observe
record

2. Selection of an interval size should provide the observer with sufficient time to reliably _____ and _____ behavior.

interval

3. Simultaneous recording of multiple behaviors and respective rates of occurrence jointly influence _____ length.

6
30

4. Interval size will usually range from _____ to _____ seconds depending on the behavior to be observed.

reliability

5. With interval recording the only criterion concerning the number of discrete behaviors or students that can be measured concurrently is _____ of recording.

one student

6. When interval recording is used for a group, observers frequently record only _____ _____ per interval.

eye contact

7. A disadvantage of using a clipboard-stopwatch timing device in interval recording is that the observer must periodically break _____ _____ with his subjects to observe the stopwatch.

a teacher-directed presentation was timed and presentation cues memorized to differentiate time intervals

8. What interval timing tactic did Jorgenson use when teaching six retarded children?

instructing
students

9. Interval recording is a measurement procedure seldom employed by classroom teachers when they are _____ _____.

frequency
duration

10. Interval recording indicates an estimate of both _____ and _____ of behavior.

across time intervals
event
duration

11. Interval recording provides an estimate of student performance _____ _____ _____ which does not occur with _____ and _____ recording.

Exercise 2–5

Pinpoint a behavior to observe. Rule a paper into squares to differentiate ten-second time intervals for a total of five minutes (thirty observation intervals). Using a stopwatch, pen, and paper, check the time intervals during which the behavior occurs. Compute the percentage of intervals in which the behavior occurred.

Time Sampling

A major disadvantage of using interval recording is that it requires the undivided attention of the observer. It is almost impossible for teachers concurrently to provide instruction and make interval recording. However, time sampling is a measurement tactic that can be used with ease by teachers while engaging in instruction. *Time sampling* is concerned with the occurrence or nonoccurrence of behaviors *immediately following* specified time intervals. Conversely, *interval recording* is concerned with behaviors *during* specified time intervals. Time sampling usually employs time intervals of minute durations (e.g. five-minute or ten-minute intervals), whereas interval recordings usually use time intervals of second durations (e.g. ten-second or twenty-second intervals).

If a teacher wishes to record the occurrence or nonoccurrence of behaviors, a paper is ruled into squares to differentiate time intervals as in interval recording. The squares may be positioned either horizontally or vertically on the paper. To record, the teacher checks time intervals in which the behavior was or was not ongoing when the interval timed out. Behavior is recorded only once per interval and reported as percent of occurrence. For example, a directive teacher is concerned with student on task behaviors during a thirty-minute seat work assignment. The thirty-minute lesson time could be divided into five-minute intervals. The teacher then observes and records the student's behavior six times during the thirty-minute seat work assignment. Observation and recording is made only at the end of each five-minute interval. Regardless of student behaviors *during* the five-minute interval, the teacher records only the student's behavior at the instant the interval timed out.

Figure 2–10 shows that the student was on task 66⅔ percent of the

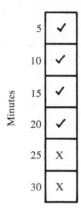

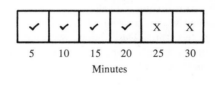

X = Student off task
✓ = Student on task

FIGURE 2–10

time during his thirty-minute seat work assignment (4 on task intervals/ 6 total intervals × 100 = 66⅔%).

A teacher can use a wall clock or a wrist watch for time sampling. However, when giving instruction it is difficult to time intervals without a signal device. Common *kitchen timers* have been found to be useful as signal devices for time sample measures. The Lux minute meter timer is an inexpensive timing device with a one-year guarantee against defects. The timer can be set at minute intervals up to one hour. A description of timers for signaling time sample intervals is found in the appendix.

Applied Example

Bushell, Wrobel, and Michaelis (1968) reported use of time sampling in a preschool class of twelve children.

> The four principal observers were seated in an observation room. Each wore earphones which enabled audio monitoring of the class and also prevented inter-observer communication. On a signal at the beginning of each 5-min period, each observer looked for the first child listed on the roster and noted that child's behavior on the data sheet, then looked for the second child on the list and noted its behavior; and so on for each child. All observers were able to complete the total observational cycle in less than 3 min. During the 75 min of observation, the children's behavior was described by noting what the child was looking at, to whom he was talking, and what he was doing with his hands. Fourteen daily observations of each child by each observer produced 672 items of data each day.

Criteria were established by which each behavioral description on the data sheets could be coded as either "S", indicating study behavior, or "NS", indicating nonstudy behavior. Behaviors such as writing, putting a piece in a puzzle, reciting to a teacher, singing a Spanish song with the class, and tracing around a pattern with a pencil were classified as "S", if they were observed in the appropriate setting. Descriptions of behaviors such as counting tokens, putting away materials, walking around the room, drinking at the fountain, looking out the window, rolling on the floor and attending to another child, were classified as "NS". Singing a Spanish song was scored "S" if it occurred during the Spanish period when called for, but "NS" if it occurred during an earlier or later period. Similarly, if one child was interacting with another over instructional materials during the study teams period, the behavior was labeled "S", but the same behavior during another period was classified "NS".

If a given child's behavior was described 14 times and eight of these descriptions were coded "S", then the amount of study time for that child was 8/14 for that day. The amount of study behavior for the entire class on a given day was the sum of the 12 individual scores. (Buschell et al. 1968)

Parameters

Time sampling is a useful tactic for the classroom teacher for he obtains numerical estimates of group or student behaviors while engaging in instruction or other activities.

Evaluation

You may choose to evaluate how well you comprehended time sampling by responding to the following test items. Cover the answer column with a sheet of paper; then write your answers in the blank spaces provided. The correct answers may then be checked.

following

1. Time sampling is concerned with the occurrence or nonoccurrence of behaviors immediately _____ specified time intervals.

during

2. Interval recording is concerned with behaviors _____ specified time intervals.

minute

3. Time sampling usually employs time intervals of _____ durations.

second

4. Interval recording usually employs time intervals of _____ durations.

timed out

5. To record with time samples, the teacher checks time intervals to indicate that behavior was or was not ongoing when the interval _____   _____.

Exercise 2–6

Observe the same behavior that was recorded in exercise 2-5 (interval recording). Rule a paper into squares to differentiate three-minute time intervals for a total of thirty minutes (ten observation intervals). Using a stopwatch, pen, and paper, check the time intervals in which the behavior was ongoing when the interval timed out. Compute the percentage of intervals in which the behavior occurred.

References

Baer, D. M., M. M. Wolf, and T. R. Risley. "Some Current Dimensions of Applied Behavior Analysis." *Journal of Applied Behavior Analysis* 1 (1968): 91–97.

Bijou, S. W., R. F. Peterson, and M. H. Ault. "A Method to Integrate Descriptive and Experimental Field Studies at the Level of Data and Empirical Concepts." *Journal of Applied Behavior Analysis* 1 (1968): 175–91.

Bushell, D. Jr., A. Wrobel, and M. L. Michaelis. "Applying 'Group' Contingencies to the Classroom Study Behavior of Preschool Children." *Journal of Applied Behavior Analysis* 1 (1968): 55–61.

Christensen, A. and J. La Barbera. "The Use of a Feedback-Reinforcement Procedure to Decrease Talking Between Two Boys in a Class for the Educationally Handicapped." In R. V. Hall, ed., *Managing Behavior, Part 3*. H & H Enterprises, P. O. Box 3342, Lawrence, Kansas, 1971.

Hall, R. V. *Managing Behavior, Part 1*. H & H Enterprises, P. O. Box 3342, Lawrence, Kansas, 1971.

Hall, R. V., D. Lund, and D. Jackson. "Effects of Teacher Attention on Study Behavior." *Journal of Applied Behavior Analysis* 1 (1968): 1–12.

Jorgenson, H. A. "Use of a Music Activity and Social Reinforcement to Increase Group Attending Behavior." Paper presented at the Fiftieth Annual International Convention of the Council for Exceptional Children, Washington, D.C., 1972.

Krauss, S. J. "Increasing Playing-Alone Behavior by Making Viewing of a Favorite Television Show Contingent on Play in a Pre-Schooler." Unpublished manuscript, Exceptional Children, Ohio State University, Columbus, Ohio, 1972.

Mattos, R. L. "Some Relevant Dimensions of Interval Recording Procedures." Working Paper #186, Parsons Research Center, Parson, Kansas 1968.

Sulzer, Beth and G. Roy Mayer. *Behavior Modification Procedures for School Personnel.* Hinsdale, Illinois: The Dryden Press, Inc., 1972.

Van Dyke, M. "Reduction of Time Spent in Drying Dishes and Number of Reprimands given by Mother During the Process by Using Positive Reinforcement." Unpublished manuscript, Exceptional Children, Ohio State University, Columbus, Ohio, 1972.

Worthy, R. C. "A Miniature, Portable Timer and Audible Signal-Generating Device." *Journal of Applied Behavior Analysis* 1 (1968): 159–60.

Wright, H. F. "Observational Child Study." In P. H. Mussen, ed., *Handbook of Research Methods in Child Development.* New York: Wiley, 1960.

Part **2**

Reporting Teaching Effects

"One hundred rumors are not comparable to one look."
—*an old Chinese inscription*

After reading and applying the measurement techniques presented in part one, you may have said, "Now that I have pinpointed and measured a behavior for specified periods of time, how will it be used in teaching?" Hopefully, part two of this book, and later part three, will answer that question. Part two is concerned with reporting teaching effects. Graphic presentation of classroom behaviors is a meaningful way for a teacher to communicate the effect of her teaching—communication not only for students, parents, and administrators, but also to illustrate clearly to herself how well students are learning. The effectiveness of graphic displays for communication can be seen by noting the use of graphs in reports from government, business, and science.

In chapter 3 the following graphic designs are presented: (1) noncumulative graph, (2) cumulative graph, (3) multiple concurrent graphics and (4) graphic presentations of central tendency and range scores.

Chapter 4 presents techniques for preparing graphs for printing. Topics in this chapter cover: (1) preparing the final copy, (2) preparing a camera copy, (3) what to do with a mistake and (4) making the photograph.

3

Graphic
Presentations

Teachers should maintain written records of student behaviors that indicate when (*units of time*) behaviors were measured, when and what intervention tactics (*instruction method*) were applied, and the *amount* of recorded behaviors. With this information, directive teachers can compare (a) behaviors across instruction periods, (b) differential effects of instruction, and (c) magnitude of behavior change. Graphic presentation of such data is a convenient convention which provides a visual comparison of behaviors across units of time and offers ease of communicating teaching effects.

Standard graphic arrangements employ two axes drawn at right angles —a horizontal axis (X-axis) and a vertical axis (Y-axis) (see figure 3–1). Usually in directive teaching, the units of measurement are *amount of behavior* (e.g. frequency, rate, percent, proportion, duration) for the Y-axis, and *units of time* (e.g. minutes, sessions, days, weeks) for the X-axis.

Graphical presentation is a much neglected teaching endeavor. The main advantage of good graphing is that it clearly allows the teacher to judge student performance and consequently teacher performance.

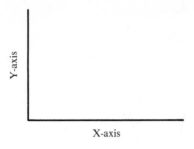

Y-axis

X-axis

FIGURE 3–1

Graphic Conventions in Directive Teaching

Noncumulative Graph

The most comon form of graphic presentation in directive teaching is the *noncumulative graph* (line graph). To construct a line graph, scores are placed on squared graph paper. The amount of behavior (Y-axis) is plotted at the intersection of the time section (X-axis). After points have been placed, they are connected by a line to form a polygon. For example, a teacher is concerned with a student who emits inappropriate talk-outs during a forty-minute fifth-grade reading class. For five consecutive days, the teacher recorded the number of inappropriate talk-out responses during reading class. The number of inappropriate talk-outs per class were 7, 9, 3, 10, and 11 occurrences. Figure 3–3 is a graphic

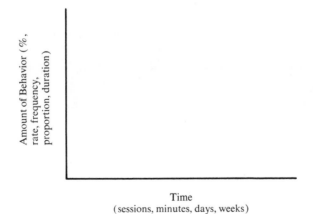

Amount of Behavior (%, rate, frequency, proportion, duration)

Time
(sessions, minutes, days, weeks)

FIGURE 3–2

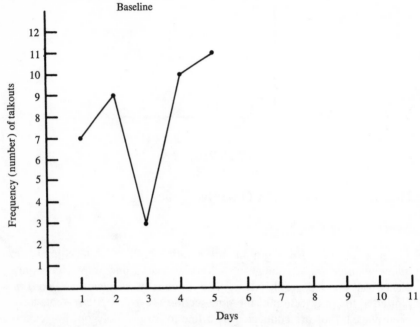

FIGURE 3–3.   *A Baseline Record of the Number of Talk-outs Emitted by a Student During a 40-Minute Fifth-grade Reading Class*

presentation of the talk-outs. All quantitative measurement (e.g. rate, frequency, percentage) can be reported with line graphs.

Exercise 3–1

Construct noncumulative graphs from the following data. Note figure 3-3 as an example.

1. Larry completed the following number of assignments during five consecutive weeks: 11, 13, 10, 9, 12.

2. Jack emitted the following number of inappropriate talk-outs during five fifteen-minute observation sessions: 10, 30, 25, 18, 11.

Cumulative Graph

Cumulative graphs are also used extensively in directive teaching. These graphs are constructed identically to the noncumulative line graph with one difference. Cumulative graphs differ from noncumulative line graphs in that the amount of behavior observed and recorded for the first session is added to the amount of behavior recorded for the second session. The sum of the first two sessions is then added to the amount of behavior occurring in the third session, etc.

For example, if the talkout data (7, 9, 3, 10, and 11 occurrences) from the hypothetical fifth-grade reading class were reported as cumulative frequencies, the graph would be constructed as shown in figure 3–4a.

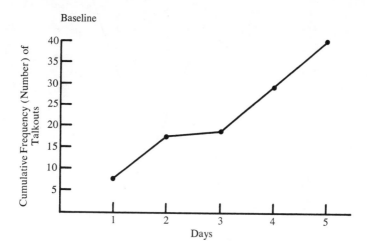

FIGURE 3–4a.   *A Baseline Record of the Cumulative Frequency of Talk-outs Emitted by a Student During a 40-Minute Fifth-grade Reading Class*

(Note the different presentations of the same data in figure 3–4a, a cumulative graph and figure 3–4b, a noncumulative graph.)

The data points for figure 3–4a were derived first by graphing the seven talkouts for day one. On day two, the student talked out nine times. Therefore, a cumulative data point for 16 occurrences (7 [day 1] and 9 [day 2] = 16) was placed on the graph. On day three, the student inappropriately talked out three times which gave a cumulative total of 18 occurrences (16 [days 1 and 2] and 3 [day 3] = 19), and so on. Figure 3-4a shows that during the five days of recorded data the student emitted 40 inappropriate talk-outs.

Exercise 3–2

Construct cumulative graphs from the data presented in exercise 3-1. Note figure 3-4a as an example of a cumulative graph.

Detailed Records with Cumulative Graphs.   Cumulative graphs are excellent for maintaining detailed records of how behaviors are occurring across time and what responses were correct or incorrect. Suppose a teacher administered spelling tests. If this teacher recorded spelling scores in percentages or frequencies she would have no record of what

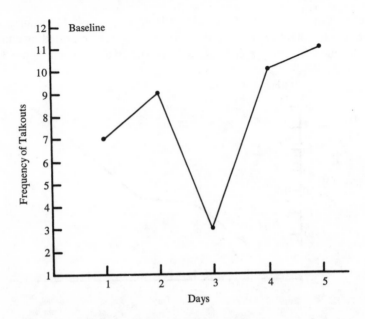

FIGURE 3–4b.   A Baseline Record of the Number of Talk-
outs Emitted by a Student During a 40-
Minute Fifth-grade Reading Class

words the student spelled correctly or incorrectly, unless she kept all tests
on file. However, filing all test responses would be cumbersome and difficult for precise comparisons of specified words across extended time
periods. A more economical convention would be to graph cumulatively
each spelling word and file only the master copy of the test. To illustrate,
suppose the teacher gave the following spelling test labeled October 13,
and the student responded as indicated (student responses October 13).

Spelling Test for October 13	Student's Responses October 13
1. boy	1. boy
2. girl	2. girl
3. house	3. house
4. horse	4. house
5. dog	5. dog
6. cat	6. cat
7. bat	7. bat
8. chair	8. char
9. table	9. table
10. eleven	10. el

Then, the student's spelling responses could be cumulatively graphed as
presented in figure 3–5.

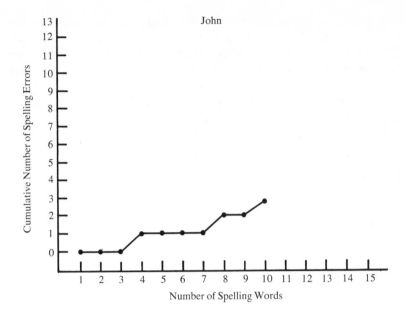

FIGURE 3–5. Cumulative Graphic Presentation of Spelling Words

This graphic presentation shows that the student answered the first three spelling words correctly; missed the fourth word; the fifth, sixth, and seventh words were spelled correctly; the eighth word was incorrect; ninth was correct; and the tenth word was incorrect. It is easy to look at the graph and immediately see that ten spelling words were given and that the student misspelled the fourth, eighth, and tenth spelling words on the list. Suppose that on the next day, the teacher gave another spelling test and the student responded as follows:

Spelling Test for October 14	*Student's Responses October 14*
1. big	1. big
2. little	2. little
3. horse	3. horse
4. up	4. up
5. down	5. down
6. June	6. June
7. July	7. July
8. eleven	8. eleven
9. chair	9. chair
10. boy	10. boy

The graphic presentation (figure 3–6) shows that on October 14 the student spelled all ten words correctly and that he has spelled a total of 20 words out of which 3 were incorrectly spelled. The student's spelling graph would continue as presented in figure 3–6. Note that (1) the hori-

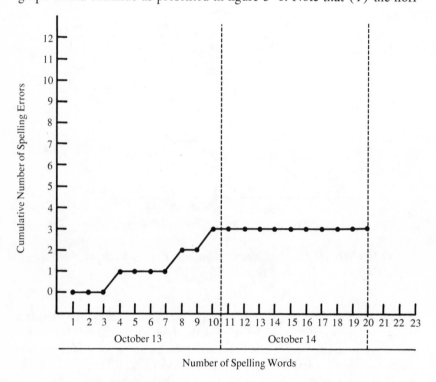

FIGURE 3–6.   *Cumulative Graphic Presentation of Spell-ing Words*

zontal base of the graph represents cumulative responses; (2) the vertical axis indicates cumulative error responses; and (3) the small vertical line above and below the dots (#10 and #20) divides responses into test sessions.

Case Study

The following case study illustrates the use of detailed cumulative graphing:

The subject of this study was a nine-year-old girl who had been enrolled in a special classroom for three years. On March 18, 1970, the student scored a 63 IQ on a Stanford-Binet intelligence test. The student did not name certain sight vocabulary words despite individualized instruction. The teacher would use flash card games during reading to encourage the student to learn to recognize certain words. The child was given the shape of a word and was instructed to match a word with its shape. Frequently, the student was asked to trace the letters and/or shape of a word and then practice printing the word. These procedures, according to the teacher, produced no behavior change.

Procedure

A multiple baseline design* (Baer, Wold, and Risley 1968) was used employing three experimental conditions: (1) baseline, (2) model and reinforcement, and (3) follow-up.

Baseline. The teacher randomly selected five words to which the student had previously been introduced but did not identify. Each of the five words was printed on five separated four-by-five-inch note cards, making twenty-five response cards. An additional fifteen cards were printed. On each of these additional cards was one word that the student had named correctly. A total of forty response cards was used in obtaining baseline data. The five words to which the student did not respond were: is, with, this, want, and they.

The teacher and student were alone in the classroom except when an independent observer also collected data. The teacher sat at a table facing the student. Prior to the session, the teacher shuffled the cards to derive a random ordering. During the session, the teacher held up one card at a time to set the occasion for a student verbal response. When the student responded, the teacher laid the card face down on the table and proceeded in identical manner with the remaining cards. No praise for correct responses or instruction for incorrect responses was given during baseline.

Data Collection. The order in which the words were randomly presented had been recorded on a data sheet previous to presenting them to the student. Incorrect responses were recorded by checking the data sheet next to the word that was incorrectly identified.

Model and Reinforcement. Model and reinforcement condition was the same as baseline with two exceptions. First, whenever the student responded incorrectly to a specified word, the teacher gave the correct

---

* See part three for a description of the multiple baseline design.

model (e.g. teacher said, "say is"). The student then imitated the verbal model. Second, for each selected verbal response that was emitted correctly, *without a verbal model setting the occasion for the response,* the teacher colored one rectangle of a series of fifteen small (approximately ¼-by-½ inch) rectangles. When the rectangle series was completely colored, the student was allowed to be the "milk carrier" that day for her classroom (reinforcement).

Follow-up.   Follow-up was a return to the original baseline conditions on 7, 15, and 21 days after the completion of training.

Results

Observer Agreements.   An observer recorded the occurrences of incorrect verbal responses by checking a separate data sheet during one session of baseline, one session of model and reinforcement, and during one of the follow-up sessions. Agreement between the teacher's recordings and that of the independent observer was 100 percent.

Figure 3–7 presents data for responses "is," "with," "this," "want," and "they" with the following conditions: (1) baseline, (2) model and reinforcement, and (3) follow-up.

Baseline.   The student incorrectly named all thirty-five occurrences of "is," all fifty occurrences of "with," all sixty-five occurrences of "this," all eighty occurrences of "want," and all ninety-five occurrences of "they."

Model and Reinforcement.   Incorrect responses decreased immediately following onset of the model and reinforcement condition. Out of eighty-five occurrences of the response "is," only two responses were incorrectly identified during the model and reinforcement contingency, one out of seventy occurrences of "with" was incorrectly identified. Five of the six incorrect responses were the first responses during the model and reinforcement condition.

Follow-up.   Follow-up data revealed that on 7, 14, and 21 days after the termination of the model and reinforcement contingency, the student responded to "is," "with," "this," "want," and "they" with 100 percent accuracy.

Exercise 3–3

Construct a detailed cumulative graph from the following data. (See figure 3–6.)

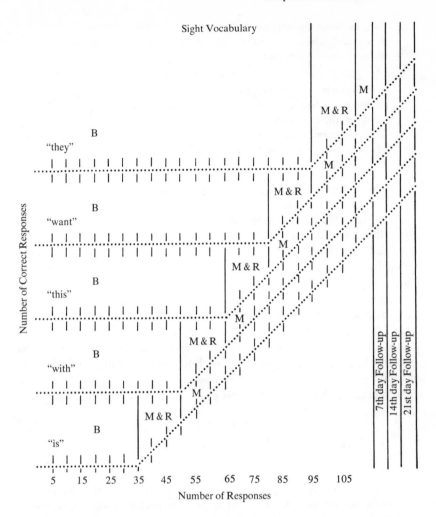

The vertical axes indicate cumulative correct responses. The small vertical line above and below the dots divides responses into sessions. *B* represents Baseline; *M & R*, Model and Reinforcement condition (Model—Teacher said, "say is," "say with," etc. contingent on an incorrect student response. Reinforcement—contingent on 15 tokens the student was "milk carrier" for her class.) *M* represents the Model condition with Reinforcement.

FIGURE 3–7. The Horizontal Base of the Graph Represents Cumulative Responses

1. Deb was learning the Dolch word list. With one of the words, "when," Deb's responses were recorded in the following way:

Session 1 (oral responses to "when")
  first response   —incorrect
  second response—incorrect

```
    third response   —correct
    fourth response —incorrect
    fifth response   —incorrect
Session 2
    first response   —incorrect
    second response—correct
    third response   —correct
    fourth response —correct
    fifth response   —correct
```

Multiple Concurrent Graphic Presentations

Frequently it will be advantageous for directive teachers to present multiple classes of data on the same graph. For example, data of more than one student, different behaviors of one student, or student and teacher behaviors. The main criterion in multiple concurrent graphics is that the data clearly show the effects of performance. A major problem encountered in this procedure is cluttered graphs that are difficult to read. A general rule is to graph no more than three classes of data on the same graph unless there is wide variation in the concurrent data points. Note that figures 3–8 and 3–9 (King 1972) report data of three students on one graph. If more data points were plotted concurrently on the graph, it would be difficult to interpret, thereby defeating the purpose of graphic representations. King illustrates this point in the following case study.

SUBJECTS

Three intermediate special students were chosen for this study. They were two males and one female, ages 9, 11, and 12 years. These students worked on academic tasks only for short periods of time. A remedial situation was instituted to increase the duration of on-task episodes and the total amount of time spent working during a fifteen minute observational period.

BEHAVIOR

The children were observed for duration of working episodes and occasions of stopping work. Working was defined as writing, reading or computing. Event and duration recordings were taken simultaneously. Using event recording, the number of times the child stopped working was tallied. The duration of each working episode was measured using a stopwatch. All observations were taken during daily fifteen minute sessions.

Inter-observer agreement checks were taken by a second, independent observer. Average agreement measures for the three children were 90%, 90%, and 85%.

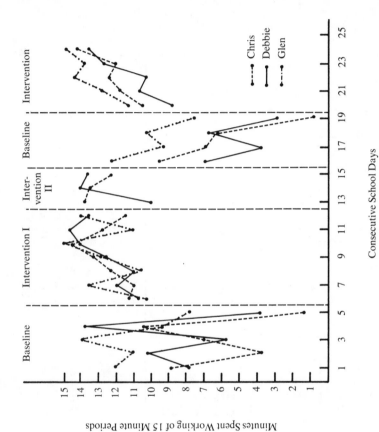

FIGURE 3–8. *A Record of the Minutes Spent Working on Writing, Reading or Computing by Three Intermediate Special Students*

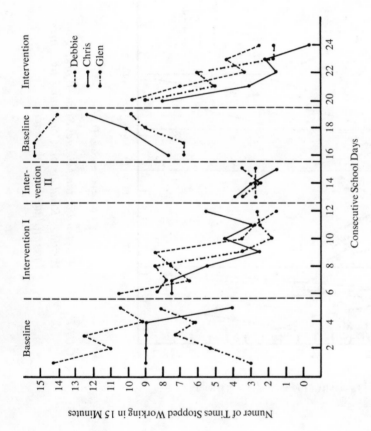

FIGURE 3–9. A Record of the Number of Times Three Intermediate Special Students Stopped Working on Writing, Reading, or Computing

PROCEDURES

Social reinforcement on a variable interval (3–10 minutes) schedule contingent on working behavior, was instituted. Other class members were selected to pass out coupons to working students. This schedule was increased to a fixed interval of 15 minutes, the reward contingent on working throughout entire sessions.

RESULTS

Following a baseline average of 8 minutes on-task, during the first intervention, the on-task average for Subject 1 increased to 13 minutes. During the second intervention, his average remained stable at 13 minutes and decreased to an average of 5 minutes when baseline conditions were again in effect. His average on task behavior increased to 12 minutes when the intervention was reinstated. Subjects 2 and 3 showed similar results.

The record of the number of stops during fifteen minutes shows a similar trend in behavior. Following a high rate during baseline, behavior decreased during the first and second interventions, increased again under baseline conditions and decreased during the reinstatement of the intervention. (King 1972)

Figure 3–10 shows a clear presentation of pre-post-test observational data in multiple concurrent presentations as reported by Arnett and Dremann (1972).

SUBJECT

In-service training in directive teaching and contingency management was instituted by the authors. Of the sixteen teachers involved in these sessions, one target subject was chosen for observation. The purpose of the observation was to determine the effectiveness of the training sessions in accomplishing the objectives of the course.

BEHAVIOR

Teacher positive and negative consequences, and student disruptive behaviors were defined (see table 3-1). These behaviors were concurrently recorded using a tally during three, five-minute intervals in a half hour during the school morning. A reliability check taken by two independent observers resulted in 86.5% agreement.

PROCEDURE

Teacher and students were observed for five days previous to the in-service training sessions, constituting pretest data. Nine training sessions followed, covering behavior and academic assessment, instructional tasks and behavioral objects, terminal behaviors and

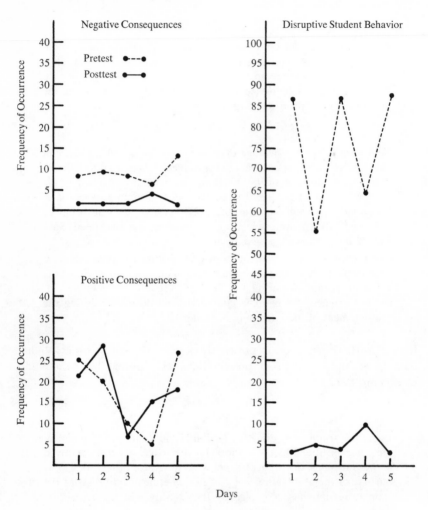

FIGURE 3-10.   Teacher Consequences and Student Disruptive Behaviors During 15 Minutes of School Mornings

criterion levels, and evaluation procedures. Following these sessions, five days of posttest data were taken.

RESULTS

The target teacher showed a decrease in her use of negative consequences from a pretest average of 8.4 occurrences in 15 minutes, to a posttest average or 1.2. Disruptive behaviors in the classroom also decreased from an average of 76 incidents in 15 minutes to an average of 5.2 during posttesting. (Arnett and Dremann 1972)

TABLE 3–1.   *Behavior Definitions*

Positive and Negative Consequences

1.	+ vocal	Verbal contact indicating approval or commendation to an individual, either loudly or softly ("that's good, fine, good job," etc.)
2.	− vocal	Verbal reprimand to an individual. This can include critical comment such as yelling, scolding, threatening (such as in mentioning consequences if certain acts happen or fail to happen) or reprimand ("sit down, get quiet," etc.)
3.	+ physical	This includes actual physical contact and close physical proximity to a child when the teacher's intent is to deal with the child in a positive way (patting, embracing, holding hand, helping with work, etc.)
4.	− physical	This includes actual physical contact and close physical proximity to a child when the teacher's intent is to deal with the child in a negative or punitive way (shaking, spanking, grabbing, standing over while lecturing, etc.)
5.	+ facial	Looking at child and smiling, nodding, winking or giving other indication of approval
6.	− facial	Looking at child and frowning or eyeing down or other indications of disapproval

Disruptive Behavior

Disruptive behavior was defined as any intentional behavior that was not purposeful to the task at hand and which caused the teacher and/or one or more students to take notice, comment, or other action in response to the behavior. The behavior was tallied under one of five forms of observable behavior:

A. Vocal, any audible behavior, e.g. talking, deliberate yawning, belching, whispering, whistling, etc.

B. Noise: any audible behavior, without permission, other than vocalization, e.g., tapping pencil, tapping of feet, moving desk, etc.

C. Out of chair: Any observable movement of the child out of chair, or out of a normal working position, e.g. walking about room, stretching out over the top of the desk, etc.

D. Play: any disruptive action to divert attention from the assigned task, e.g. playing with a toy, comb, cleaning fingernails, including drawing or reading of non-task materials

E. Aggression: any threatening action toward another person, e.g. hitting, leaning or otherwise touching student, pulling chair away, taking papers, books or pencils, etc.

The directive teacher may be concerned with both duration and frequency of behavioral events (e.g. the duration of minutes in time-out and the number of times placed in time-out). In such cases where both frequency and duration may be graphed together, a combination line and bar graph is a useful tactic to show behavior change. To illustrate, suppose a student demonstrated high durations of nonattending behavior during daily 30-minute seat work periods. The teacher's strategy for decelerating nonattending behaviors was to reinforce attending behaviors that were incompatible with nonattending responses. The number of attending behaviors that were reinforced was gradually reduced as the target behavior came under control of the contingency. Duration of nonattending behavior and number of reinforcers presented are given in table 3–2 for seven days of intervention (reinforcement of attending

TABLE 3–2. *Duration of Nonattending Behavior and Number of Reinforcers*

	Study Period Sessions	Duration in Minutes of Nonattending Behavior	Number of Reinforcers Presented for Attending (on Task)
INTERVENTION	10	20	15
	11	18	15
	12	15	8
	13	7	6
	14	5	4
	15	2	1
	16	2	1

behaviors). Figure 3–11 gives a graphic representation of the minutes of nonattending behavior per session and the number of reinforced attending responses.

Reporting Central Tendency and Range Scores

Directive teachers typically instruct groups of students. Often group data will be used to describe classroom performance. In describing a group performance, directive teachers should indicate the *central tendency* (i.e. a representative value for the classroom performance) and the *range* of the data. Measures of central tendency and indication of the spread of scores can be depicted with graphic methods.

Common Measures of Central Tendency: The Mean, Median

The *mean* is the most common measure of central tendency. It is an arithmetic average of a set of data. If, for example, a teacher wished to determine the average score of a group of students on an addition test, she would sum the individual scores and divide that sum by the number of measurements. This procedure generates an average score which is

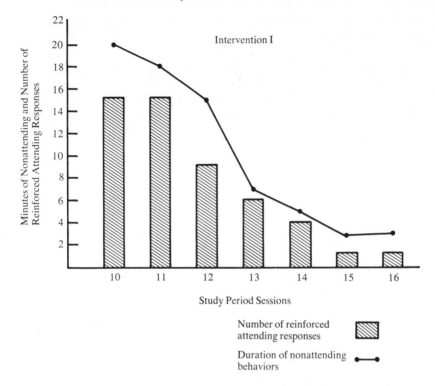

Reinforcement of Incompatible Behavior

FIGURE 3–11. Duration of Nonattending Behaviors and Number of Reinforcers Presented During Seven Days of Intervention

called the mean. As an illustration, eleven students emitted the following number of correct responses on an addition test: 10, 15, 15, 13, 9, 7, 5, 11, 12, 10, 10.

$$\frac{\text{sum of the numbers}}{\text{number of measurements}} = \frac{117}{11} = 10.7 = \text{arithmetic mean}$$

The *median* is another measure of central tendency. The median is the middle score in a ranked distribution. It is that point which divides a group into two equal groups—a lower half and an upper half. For example, to derive the median point of the addition test scores from the eleven students, first place the scores in rank order, i.e. 5, 7, 9, 10, 10, 10, 11, 12, 13, 15, 15. Second, find the middle score that divides the measurements into two equal groups (figure 3–12a). The middle point or median is 10, with five scores occurring below and five scores occurring above the median. If the distribution is an odd number of scores, the median is usually easy to determine. However, suppose the teacher only had the following 10 scores from the addition test: 7, 9, 10, 10, 10, 11, 12, 13, 15, 15. In this case, when the distribution is divided into lower and upper groups, there is no score to divide the groups (figure 3–12b). The last score of the lower group is 10 and the first score of the upper group is 11, therefore, a median point is placed midway between 10 and 11, at 10.5, even though no student had an addition score of 10.5 (figure 3-12c).

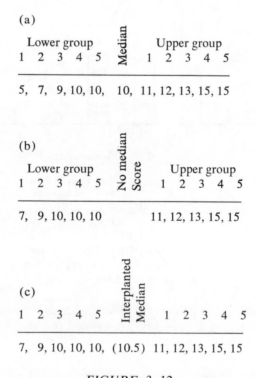

FIGURE 3–12

Appropriate Use of the Mean, Median.   The mean and median points for the hypothetical addition test data were very similar (i.e. 10.7 mean, 10.5 median). However, that is not always the case. Ordinarily the mean will be the best index of central tendency. But, if a few scores are exaggerated—extremely high or extremely low—in comparison to the group, then the median would be a good index of central tendency. Suppose a teacher wished to know typically how long it took her class to "settle down" to on task behavior following entry to the classroom after morning recess. Individual student scores in duration of time to on task were: 10 sec., 10 sec., 13 sec., 15 sec., 15 sec., 180 sec., which gave a mean of 37.6 seconds. It is obvious that the 37.6 seconds mean does not provide an adequate picture of the "typical" classroom behavior. The exaggerated score of 180 seconds inflated the mean score. Conversely the median of 14 seconds does give a better description of the total class behavior.

Range

The range score is the difference between the lowest and highest score in a set of measurements. The range score of the hypothetical addition test data used to illustrate computation of the mean is 10 (table 3–3).

TABLE 3–3

Addition Test Scores	Calculation of Range
5	15 = the highest score in the
7	distribution
9	— 5 = the lowest score in the
10	distribution
10	10 = Range score
10	
11	
12	
13	
15	
15	

Only two scores are used to calculate the range. Therefore, range scores cannot show how individual scores are spread in a distribution. Range scores are used in directive teaching only to show the upper and lower scores of a class. Usually, in presenting the range of a class on a graph, both the upper and lower scores are graphed rather than the range score.

Graphic Presentation of Central Tendency and Range

Suppose we have the following data from a class performance of addition problems for one week:

Days	= 1	2	3	4	5	6
Mean	= 10	9	12	15	15	15
Spread	= 5–15	8–17	3–20	9–20	10–20	10–20

A graphic presentation of this data is figure 3–13.

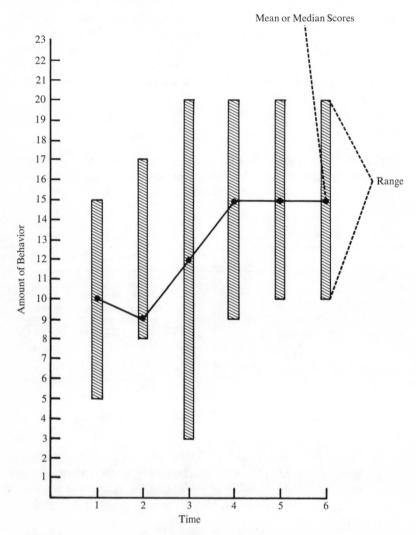

FIGURE 3–13.   Example of Graphing Central Tendency
and Range Scores

Evaluation

You may choose to evaluate how well you comprehend reporting teaching effects by responding to the following test items. Cover the answer column with a sheet of paper; then write your answers in the blank spaces provided. The correct answers may then be checked.

behaviors across
  instruction periods
differential effects of
  instruction
magnitude of behavior
  change

1. When directive teachers maintain written records of student behaviors that indicate *when* behaviors were measured, *when and what* instructional methods were applied, and the *amount* of recorded behaviors they can compare:

   a.
   b.
   c.

2. Standard graphic arrangements employ two axes drawn at right angles. Identify these axes.

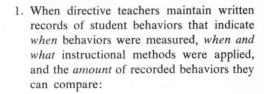

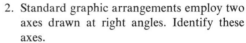

amount
behavior

3. Usually in directive teaching, the units of measurement reported on the Y-Axis are _____ of _____.

units of time

4. Usually the units of measurement reported on the X-Axis are _____ _____.

student performance

5. The main advantage of good graphing is that it clearly allows the teacher to judge _____ _____ and consequently teacher performance.

noncumulative

6. The most common form of graphic presentation in directive teaching is the _____ graph.

directive teaching

7. Cumulative graphs are also used extensively in _____ _____.

Cumulative graphs

8. _____ _____ are excellent for maintaining detailed records of how behaviors are occurring across time and what responses were correct or incorrect.

central tendency
range

9. In describing a group performance, directive teachers should indicate the _____ _____ and the _____ of the data.

mean   10. The _____ is an arithmetic
                        average of a set of data.

median   11. The _____ is the middle score
                        in a ranked distribution.

mean   12. Ordinarily the _____ will be
median   the best index of central tendency. But, if
                        a few scores are extremely high or low the
                        _____ should be used.

range   13. The _____ score is the differ-
                        ence between the lowest and highest scores
                        in a set of measurements.

Points to Remember in Making Graphic Presentations

Verbal descriptions written on the graph should be brief yet complete
enough so that the graph conveys information concerning the pinpointed
behavior, teaching tactic, and results without making recourse to other
sources of explanation. To illustrate, what statements can be made from
the data in figure 3–14 (adapted from Crisp 1972)? Little information
is given in figure 3–14. The only statements that can be made are that
some type of answers emitted by a seven-year-old student were recorded,
that something changed during treatment condition (but we do not
know what), and that the data were accumulated over twenty-eight days.

Now consider the information in figure 3–15 (Crisp 1972). Figure
3–15 provides information upon which instructional decisions can be
made by the student's teacher or other interested personnel (e.g. other
teachers, parents, ancillary school personnel, etc.).

First, we see that the pinpointed behavior was volunteering and an-
swering teacher questions by raising hand. Second, we see that during
baseline the teacher asked, on the average, approximately seventeen
questions during nine daily ten-minute segments of language arts period.
During this condition, the student did not answer any questions.

Third, when the teacher intervened by having the student self-record
the number of times he volunteered to answer questions, and the teacher
praised him contingent upon his answers to her questions, the student's
behavior changed. In this condition, the teacher asked, on the average,
approximately nineteen questions during eighteen daily ten-minute segments of language arts period. The students' pinpoint increased from
zero answers during baseline to a daily average of seventeen answers.
Fourth, these data show that a large magnitude of positive change in the
pinpointed behavior has been demonstrated and that the teacher's intervention tactic was at least not ineffective.

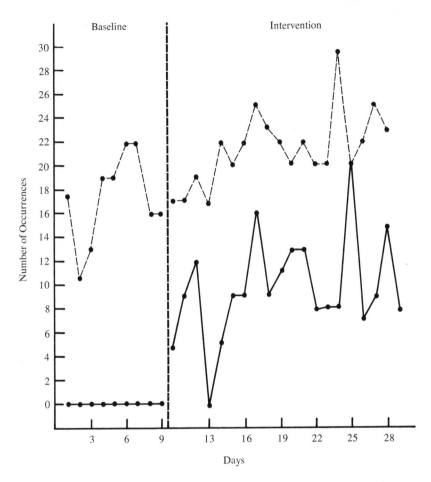

FIGURE 3–14. Number of Answers of a Seven-Year-Old
Student

Clearly, data reported in figure 3–15 are more acceptable than figure 3–14. Figure 3–15 meets some criteria of acceptable graphic presentation by conveying information concerning the behavioral pinpoint, the teaching tactic, and results of the teaching tactic without the viewer making recourse to other sources of explanations.

Some final points to remember in graphic presentations are:
1. vertical lines on the graph divide, or show changes in, teaching tactics. This point is illustrated in figure 3–16.
2. Data points between teaching phases, as indicated by vertical lines, are not joined. This second suggestion is shown in figure 3–17.

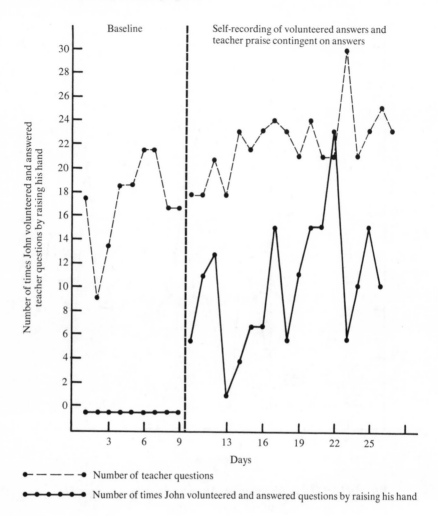

FIGURE 3–15.   *Record of a Seven-Year-Old Boy's An-*
swers to Teacher's Questions During a
10-Minute Language Arts Period

3. Post-checks are graphed when a behavior is periodically measured after the teacher has formally terminated training for that
particular behavior. When graphing post-checks, do not join the
data points. Graphic procedures for post-checks are presented
in figure 3–18.

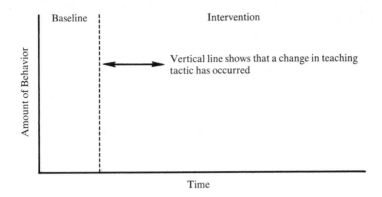

FIGURE 3-16.   *Illustration of Vertical Lines in Graphic Presentations*

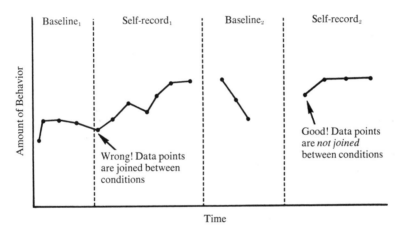

FIGURE 3-17.   *Illustration of Joining Data Points in Graphic Presentations*

Evaluation

You may choose to evaluate how well you comprehend reporting teaching effects by responding to the following test items. Cover the answer column with a sheet of paper; then write your answers in the blank spaces provided. The correct answers may then be checked.

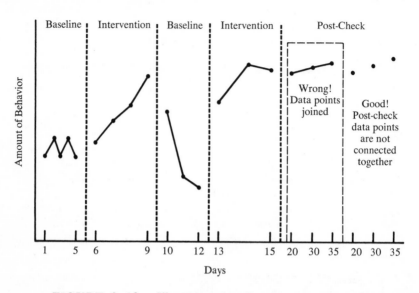

FIGURE 3–18.   Illustration for Graphic Procedures for Post-Checks

pinpointed behavior
teaching tactic
results

1. Verbal descriptions written on the graph should be brief yet complete enough so that the graph conveys information concerning the _____ _____, _____ _____, and _____ without recourse to other sources of explanation.

teaching tactics

2. Vertical lines on the graph divide, or show changes in, _____ _____.

joined

3. Data points between teaching phases, as indicated by vertical lines, are not _____.

join

4. When graphing post-checks do not _____ the data points.

References

Arnett, B. and A. K. Dremann. "Project Breakthrough Report." Unpublished manuscript, Exceptional Children, Ohio State University, Columbus, Ohio, 1972.

Baer, D. M., M. M. Wolf, and T. R. Risley. "Some Current Dimensions of Applied Behavior Analysis." *Journal of Applied Behavior Analysis* 1 (1968): 91–97.

Crisp, E. M. "From Ohio Learning Disability Project." Unpublished manuscript, Exceptional Children, Ohio State University, Columbus, Ohio 1972.

King, J. "Project Breakthrough Report." Unpublished manuscript, Exceptional Children, Ohio State University, Columbus, Ohio, 1972.

4

Preparing for Printing*

Occasionally a teacher may develop a directive teaching project so successful that it interests other professionals. Making information available to other professionals involves clear, precise writing, and neat, self-explanatory graphs, ready for printing. After the writing is finished and the last, last-minute changes made on the graphs, the author is ready to make final graphs for photographing.

Preparing the Final Graph

Final graphs are usually made in proportion, the vertical (Y) axis being two-thirds the length of the horizontal (X) axis. If the article will be submitted to a professional journal, the column space requirements should be kept in mind. Graphs are usually shown in a single column,

* This section was written by Twila Johnson, Research Associate, Exceptional Children, Ohio State University and is reproduced by permission of the author.

measuring 2⅝ inches wide (maximum length of the X-axis). Some journals request that graph labels and legends be included in the white space within the axis. In planning the final graph, sizes of letters, symbols, and widths of lines should be large enough that they can be seen when reduced to journal size. The first step then, is to draw in dark pencil (on graph paper) a final graph, in correct proportions.

For the next step, one ideally would use a lighted drafting table. However, as few teachers are also engineers, a hard, but *very* well-lighted table will do. Tape the graphs directly on the table, then center over it plain white paper so that the graph appears through the paper, centered on the page. The paper that the graph will be transferred to should be durable, shiny surfaced tracing paper (Doric Sketch Pad, by Keuffel and Esser, Co. #12-5555 is good). All drawing equipment is available from drafting supply stores (look in the yellow pages under "Drafting Room Equipment and Supplies").

Preparing Camera Copy

At this point, the author has a choice of two methods to prepare the camera copy: pen and ink, or dry-press transfer.

Pen and Ink

Pen and ink drawing produces a neat copy, but requires skill and some expensive equipment.

Pens. Pens can be purchased as the nib only (Leroy pens, by Keuffel and Esser Co.) or a reservoir pen (Koh-l-Noor Rapidograph). The reservoir pen is recommended for neater lettering.

Different sizes (line widths) of pens will be needed; a wide line for drawing the axis, narrower pens for the lettering and lines. See figure 4–1 for a guide to pen sizes.

The equipment is used together to produce letters of uniform size and design. The lettering guide is placed in the guide holder, which has been squared up with the paper. Point A of the scriber shown in figure 4–2 is placed in the letter guide as in figure 4–3 of the desired letter. Any up and down adjustment in the lettering guide and holder is then made to place the letter in the correct place on the page. With a very steady hand, move point "A" around the inside edges of the letter on the lettering guide. For some letters, the lettering guide must be moved to complete the letter, as shown in figure 4–4. Needless to say, some practice is necessary before attempting camera copy.

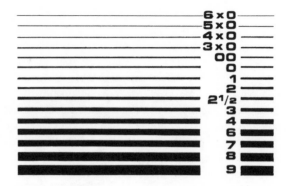

FIGURE 4-1.   Pen Size and Line Width

FIGURE 4-2.   Scriber

FIGURE 4-3.   Lettering Guide

FIGURE 4-4.   Constructing a Two-Part Letter

For an idea of the pen size and appropriate lettering guide for the desired letter height, see figure 4-5.

What to Do for a Mistake.   Brush over the mistake with a white correcting fluid, which contains toluene. If the correction fluid does not

Rapidoguide Number	Height Of Letter	For Use With Rapidograph Or Acetograph Pen
3030A	5/64″	No. 00
3030B	1/8″	No. 00
3030	5/32″	No. 0
3031	3/16″	No. 1
3032	1/4″	No. 2
3032A	9/32″	No. 2¹/₂
3033	5/16″	No. 3
3034	3/8″	No. 4
3035-6	15/32″	No. 6
3035-7	9/16″	No. 7
3035-8	5/8″	No. 8
3035-9	3/4″	No. 9

FIGURE 4–5. Guide to Pen and Letter Size

contain toluene, the mistake will appear in the photograph. Two choices for correcting fluid are Correctette and Liquid Re-Type.

Dry Press Transfer

Dry press transfer is much easier than pen and ink for the beginner and usually produces a camera-ready copy on the first try. Letters and lines are always of consistent size and easily placed. Besides all these advantages, your hands don't get soiled with ink.

Equipment. Everything necessary to make the camera copy comes on individual ten-by-fifteen-inch sheets; unfortunately, you must buy the entire sheet, which means you may have more than you need. But save it. You'll use it for something. Dry press transfer equipment is also available at drafting supply stores.

Letters. Letters come in many sizes and typefaces. They are sized according to a point system; 72 points to one inch. For the major labeling on the graph, 18 point letters are a good size for reduction, and 10 or 12 point letters for labeling the axis. For a sampling of appropriate typefaces and companies that make them, see figure 4–6. Other companies providing similar typefaces are Chartpac and Paratone.

Numbers. Numbers are sized the same as letters. Ten or 12 point numbers reduce well when numbering the axis. In some letter typefaces, the numbers are on the same page with the letters; in others, the

Normatype® Transfer Letters

Folio Bold Condensed

ABCDEFGHIJKLMNOPQRSTUVWXYZ
ÆŒÇØ 1234567890 ?!(%)&
abcdefghijklmnopqrstuvwxyz
æœçøß «»;:/.·-·-·

Haas Helvetica Medium

ABCDEFGHIJKLMNOPQRS
TUVWXYZÆŒÇØ abcdefgh
ijklmnopqrstuvwxyzæœçøß
1234567890?!(%)&«»;:/„·-·-

Grotesque No. 9

ABCDEFGHIJKLMNOPQRSTUVWX
YZÆŒÇØ 1234567890
abcdefghijklmnopqrstuvwxyz
æœçøß ?!(%)&«»;:/„"·-·

Franklin Gothic

ABCDEFGHIJKLMNOPQRS
TUVWXYZÆŒÇØ abcdefg
hijklmnopqrstuvwxyzæœç
øß1234567890?!(&);:/„·-·-·

Folio Medium Extended Italic

ABCDEFGHIJKLMNOP
QRSTUVWXYZÆŒÇØ
abcdefghijklmnopqrst
uvwxyzæœçøß
1234567890?!()«»;:/„"·-·-·

Futura Bold

ABCDEFGHIJKLMNOPQ
RSTUVWXYZÆŒÇØ
abcdefghijklmnopqrstu
vwxyzæœçøß «»;:/·-~··
1234567890?!() ·

Letraset
33 New Bridge Road, Bergenfield, New Jersey 07621

Grotesque 9 Italic

ABCDEFGHIJK
LMNOPQRSTUVWXYZ
abcdefghijkl
mnopqrstuvwxyz
1234567890
&?!ß£$()

Folio Medium Ext.

ABCDEFGHIJKLM
NOPQRSTUVWXYZ
abcdefghijkl
mnopqrstuvwxyz
1234567890
&?!ß£$()

Standard Medium

ABCDEFGHIJKL
MNOPQRSTUVWXYZ
abcdefghijkl
mnopqrstuvwxyz
1234567890
?!&()

ENGINEERING STANDARD

ABCDEFGHIJKLM
NOPQRSTUVWXYZ
1234567890
&?!$();

FIGURE 4–6. *Available Typefaces by Brand Name*

94

numbers are separate. Check before buying. If your graphs call for many numbers, or several of one number (such as 5s and 0s) it is usually better to buy an entire page of numbers.

Lines.   The axis lines should be the heaviest (about 3 points) and the lines within the graph narrower (one point). Broken and dotted lines to show more than one measure on a single graph are also available. Lines are available from some companies in a roll.

Symbols.   Asterisks, stars, squares, etc., to represent data points may be purchased in varying sizes, usually with several sizes of several symbols on one page. Simply choose a size that conforms with the lettering.

To use dry press materials, place the page on the paper, centering the letter. Then with a pencil or pen scribble over the back of the entire letter. The letter will turn gray when it is released from the plastic page. After all letters are correct and in place, rub them again with the backing sheet for firm adhesion.

What to Do for a Mistake.   Erase the mistake with clean pencil eraser or scrape it off with a sharp knife.

Making the Photograph.   Printers usually require glossy prints of graphs to be published. The reduced photographs can be made by most newspaper or job printing establishments. Prices for this service vary; it might be wise to call for estimates.

That makes everything ready for publication—*Congratulations!!*

Part 3

Analytic Teaching

"Instead of speaking of 'control groups,'
we speak of 'control procedures'."
—Donald L. Whaley and
Richard W. Malott

Directive teachers are concerned with developing the technology of teaching. With this concern, it is not sufficient just to know that children have acquired certain skills during a course of instruction. The crucial question directive teachers must ask is: "What did I do as a teacher that *caused* the behavior change?" This question can be answered only in the classroom with *analytic teaching*. Analytic teaching is the educational process of demonstrating what student behavior is emitted in both the presence and absence of the teacher's instruction procedures. Further, it is desirable to demonstrate that the teacher's instruction procedures are responsible for the occurrence or nonoccurrence of specific student behavior. This section addresses the topic of tactics for analytic teaching. The following designs are presented: (1) A-B design, (2) reversal (ABAB) design, (3) variations on the reversal design and (4) multiple baseline designs.

5

Evaluation Designs
for Teachers

In the introduction to part one, the statement was made that "evaluation is based on measurement which is the way to determine student growth." This statement is true because measurement procedures will document how much a student's behavior changed. Also, measurement will tell us when our teaching is ineffective. But measurement procedures alone cannot document when our teaching is effective. "Measurement can tell us that the student has improved, but even reliable measurement of improvement does not by itself indicate what caused the improvement" (Risley 1969).

Demonstrating what teaching procedures caused a student to improve has been difficult for teachers. For, unlike measurement tactics with a well-developed methodology already established, evaluation designs that demonstrate causality with individual students or individual groups have only recently been introduced to public school education. All evaluation designs presented in chapter 5 start with a baseline logic for evaluating the effectiveness of classroom instruction on student behavior. "Baseline logic comprises one question: 'Does a treatment condition substantially affect the baseline rate of a student's behavior?' To 'affect a behavior' means not only that a change in the behavior occurs but also that we have sufficient information to attribute that change in behavior to our treatment condition" (Wolf and Risley 1969).

A-B Design

Perhaps the first classroom applications of the baseline logic used a procedure called the A-B design. The A-B design has two conditions:

1. Pretest or baseline period (repeated measures before intervention)
2. Measurement during the intervention or instruction strategy.

Figure 5–1 provides a graphic prototype of the A-B design.

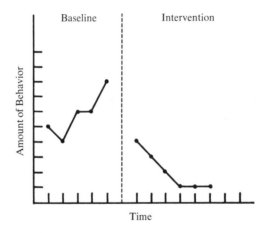

FIGURE 5–1. Prototype of the A-B Design

Directive teachers use the following steps when employing an A-B design.

1. Assess social and academic skills. Teachers not familiar with classroom assessment should read: Stephens, T. M. *Directive Teaching of Children with Learning and Behavioral Handicaps.* Columbus, Ohio: Charles E. Merrill, 1970.
Stephens, T. M. *Implementing Behavioral Approaches in Elementary and Secondary Schools.* Columbus, Ohio: Charles E. Merrill, 1974.

2. *Pinpoint* and *define* the behavior to be modified. For example:

The *pinpoint*—Talking-out

Behaviorally defined—Talking-out is defined as a vocalization, comment, or audible vocal noise initiated by the student. It cannot be in response to the teacher or another peer. Each occasion will be tallied as one talk-out, if they are separated by a breath, time interval, or change of topic.

3. Specify the *terminal behavior*. For example:

The *terminal behavior*—Given a ten-minute segment of language arts, social studies, class discussion, or seatwork assignments, the student will emit 50 percent (or fewer) of the number of talk-outs emitted prior to the implementation of the instruction variable.

4. *Select* an appropriate *measurement tactic*. For example: event, duration, interval, or time sample recording.

BASELINE
5. Measure the occurrence or nonoccurrence of the target behavior for, usually, five or more measurement periods. Following five or more measurement periods, the directive teacher should proceed to Intervention (step 6) only if the baseline measurement is *stable*. That is, when you look at your graph there is no major up or down trend in the data. However, during baseline a student's behavior may be consistently improving or regressing. In such cases the teacher may not want to start instruction until there is an asymptote trend in the data. Hall (1971) commented on this point. "John's rate of working math problems correctly is increasing. Therefore, if new [teaching] procedures were introduced to increase his math proficiency, even though he did work more problems correctly, the . . . [teacher] would not be able to determine if the . . . [new teaching] procedures were responsible for the change" (p. 13). Furthermore, Hall stated: "[Teaching] procedures can sometimes be started when a baseline is ascending, if the intent is to *decrease* the strength of the behavior, or, conversely, to begin . . . teaching procedures when a baseline is descending, if the intent is to *increase* the strength of the be-

havior. This is often done in cases where it is desirable to reverse the trend of the behavior—for example, when a child is hitting his peers at an obviously increasing rate and the desire is to decrease the hitting behavior as quickly as possible" (Hall 1971, p. 14).

INTERVENTION

6. Apply the *instruction strategy*.
7. *Discontinue instruction* after behavior has reached the terminal criteria.

POST-CHECK

8. Following the formal termination of instruction, occasionally measure the pinpointed behavior to see if the skill is still approximating the terminal criteria.

Applied Example

The following case study demonstrates an application of the A-B design.

SUBJECT

The subject was a twelve-year-old male in fifth grade. He was reading on a third grade level and had not made progress for the previous year and a half. The child was selected for this study because he demonstrated very slow academic growth and very poor study habits.

BEHAVIOR

On-task behavior was defined for this study as attention directed to the activity for fifteen minutes without putting his head down, covering work, or talking to others. Using a stopwatch, the cumulative amount of time directed toward the assigned task was recorded during a fifteen minute period. Reliability was taken by the aide in the classroom, resulting in reliability figures of 80%, 100%, 90% and 100% on the 3rd, 4th, and 6th days of the study.

PROCEDURES

Following baseline observations, a contingency management system was instituted in which the subject received five minutes of the teacher's undivided attention, contingent on fifteen minutes on-task behavior.

RESULTS

During baseline, the subject averaged ten minutes on-task. After the contingency was instituted, the subject averaged 14.5 minutes on-task, earning the reward on twelve occasions. (Wilson 1972)

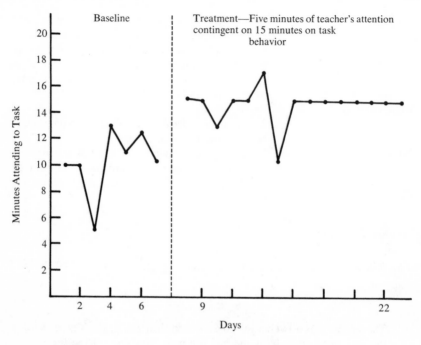

FIGURE 5–2.   *Minutes Attending to Assigned Activities*
of a 12-year-old Fifth-Grade Student

Parameters

The teacher can make statements concerning the ineffectiveness of instruction when using an A-B design. But, she cannot make statements concerning causality of a behavior change or effectiveness of instruction. For example, in the previous study by Wilson, variables other than contingent teacher attention may have accelerated on-task behavior. Perhaps the activities were more interesting or the parents intervened in some way. Numerous explanations could be proposed. Even though the student met the teacher's terminal criteria, the teacher should not say that her teaching tactic was effective. We just do not know. However, the teacher would know that her instruction tactic was ineffective if the student's behavior remained unchanged in both the baseline and teaching conditions.

To illustrate, suppose that Wilson's data appeared as reported in figure 5–3. In this hypothetical example, Wilson would know that her instruction tactic was ineffective since duration of on-task behavior was not increased. Data have been collected which can be used for teacher

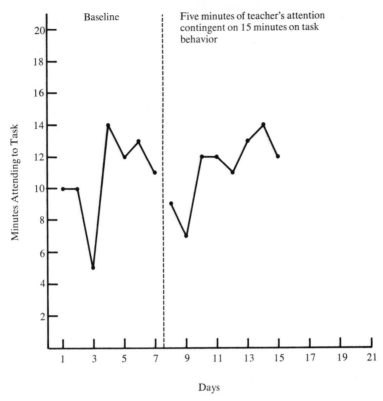

FIGURE 5-3. Hypothetical Example Demonstrating Ineffective Instruction

decisions on changing instruction methods. Therefore, this design is most useful in providing information on when to change instruction. Most data in applied behavioral analysis (e.g. see *Journal of Applied Behavior Analysis,* 1968, to date) show that if a change in behavior is to occur, the change comes in the first few training sessions. The implication for classroom teaching is that if a student has not acquired, or improved upon, the skill to be taught in one week of instruction the teacher should change her teaching procedures. Perhaps the instruction materials should be modified, or the task presented in smaller steps, or the consequence (reinforcement) of behavior changed.

Basically then, the A-B design can establish whether or not the student's behavior changed and can give an indication of the magnitude of change. Conversely, this design cannot establish effective teaching for it does not provide controlled demonstrations of causality. The student's behavior may have changed without the implementation of the instruction procedures.

Evaluation

You may choose to evaluate how well you comprehend analytic teaching by responding to the following test items. Cover the answer column with a sheet of paper; then write your answers in the blank spaces provided. The correct answers may then be checked.

baseline intervention	1. What are the two conditions associated with A-B design? a. b.
defined	2. Before selecting a measurement tactic the behavior must be _____ in observable terms.
baseline	3. Measurement before instruction or intervention is called _____ measurement.
five	4. Baseline is ongoing for usually _____ or more measurement peroids.
stable (asymptote)	5. The teacher should not introduce new teaching procedures until baseline data is _____.
where it is desirable to reverse the trend of the behavior	6. When may it be desirable to introduce new teaching procedures even though baseline is not stable? a.
false	7. The A-B design can demonstrate effectiveness of instruction. a. True b. False
ineffectiveness	8. The teacher can make statements concerning the _____ of instruction when using an A-B design.
changed magnitude	9. The A-B design can establish whether or not the student's behavior _____ and give indication of the _____ of change.

Exercise 5–1

Graph a hypothetical example of an A-B design.

Reversal Design

The A-B design is incomplete for a behavioral analysis in that it does not provide information concerning what the student's behavior would have been had the teacher not introduced her teaching procedure. One evaluation design that makes a reasonable estimate of what the student's behavior would have been had the teacher not intervened is the reversal or ABAB design. With this design, the teacher can demonstrate that her teaching was effective.

The reversal design (ABAB) has four conditions:

1. Pretest or baseline period (measurement before intervention)
2. Measurement during the intervention or instruction strategy
3. Return to baseline conditions
4. Reinstate instruction strategy.

Figure 5–4 provides a graphic prototype of the reversal design.

Directive teachers use the following steps when employing a reversal design.

1. *Assess* social and academic skills.

2. *Pinpoint* and *define* the behavior to be modified.

3. Specify the *terminal behavior.*

4. *Select* an appropriate *measurement tactic.*

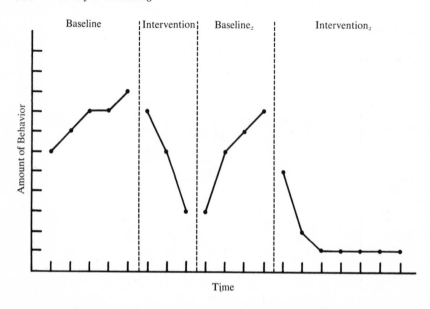

FIGURE 5–4.   Prototype of the Reversal Design

BASELINE$_1$

5. *Measure* the occurrence or nonoccurrence of the target behavior for, usually, five or more measurement periods.

INTERVENTION$_1$

6. *Apply* the instruction strategy.

   Note: Intervention$_1$ should be operative only until a trend toward the terminal criteria is observed, usually three to five training sessions.

BASELINE$_2$

7. Return to baseline$_1$ conditions.

   Note: The purpose of this condition is to demonstrate that in the absence of the intervention$_1$ procedure, behavior in baseline$_2$ will again approximate the magnitude of behavior recorded in baseline$_1$. With this operation the teacher is demonstrating causality. That is, she may demonstrate an increase in the probability that the behavior change was a result of her instruction rather than other variables. This condition is operative for a very short period of time (possibly three to five sessions).

INTERVENTION₂   8. Reinstate instruction strategy.

    9. *Discontinue instruction* after behavior has reached the terminal criteria.

POST-CHECK   10. Following the formal termination of instruction, occasionally measure the pinpointed behavior to see if the skill is still approximating the terminal criteria.

Applied Example

SUBJECT

A twelve-year-old student, who frequently talked-out in class, was chosen for this study. He exhibited mimicking behaviors and disrupted the class.

BEHAVIOR

Talking-out was defined as a vocalization, comment or audible vocal noise initiated by the student. It could not be in response to the teacher or another peer. Each occasion was tallied as one talk-out, if they were separated by a breath, time interval, or change in topic. This behavior was recorded from 9:30 to 9:40 A.M. Reliability checks were taken by two independent observers; all resulted in reliability figures between 90 and 100 per cent.

PROCEDURE

After baseline, the teacher instructed the class, "Let's see how many can talk only after raising their hands and being called upon." She then chose a student exhibiting the desired behavior, and told him, "Good, _____, you raised your hand before saying a thing."

She then immediately chose the target student for the next class contribution, and verbally praised him. From then on, she reinforced the target child on all occasions of the desired behavior, and intermittently repeated the class instruction.

Baseline conditions were reinstated. After the second baseline, instructions and praise were again in effect.

RESULTS

Following a high rate of talking-out during baseline, instruction and praise brought about a much lower rate. The behavior recovered to its high rate during baseline₂ conditions, but was again brought under control when contingencies were in effect. (Priser 1972)

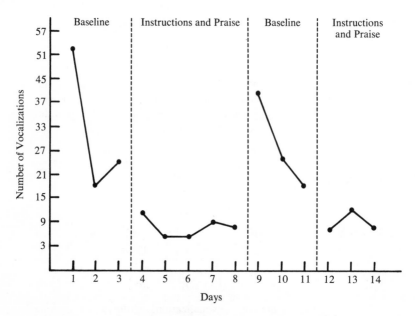

FIGURE 5–5.   Number of Classroom Talkouts of a
Twelve-year-old Student

Variations on the Reversal Design

Three variations on the reversal design logic have appeared in the literature. Each of the variations exhibits common features. First, each variation may show whether a given stimulus consequent to a behavior had
or had not *affected* that *behavior*. Second, once a consequential stimulus
is presented (reinforcement), the analysis does not call for the removal
of that stimulus condition but rather a rearrangement of the contingency. Third, each variation will demonstrate causality. These variations are:

1. the application of noncontingent reinforcement as a control
   condition;
2. the application of contingent reinforcement to a polar behavior
   of a previously reinforced behavior as a control condition; and
3. differential reinforcement of other behavior (DRO) as a control
   condition.

Noncontingent Reinforcement as a Control Factor

This application is an excellent design for demonstrating causality of a
behavior change if the intervention tactic is the contingent application

of social stimuli (reinforcement) (e.g. standing near the student, smiling, laughing, verbal praise, etc.). A frequent hypothesis advanced to explain behavior change generated from social reinforcement is that the behavior change resulted from an improved student-teacher relationship rather than the contingent response-reinforcement arrangement. It is argued by some that it would not matter how the teacher's praise and attention were given just as long as the student was in a warm, loving, accepting environment. The design prototype in figure 5–6 isolates the analysis of contingent relationships.

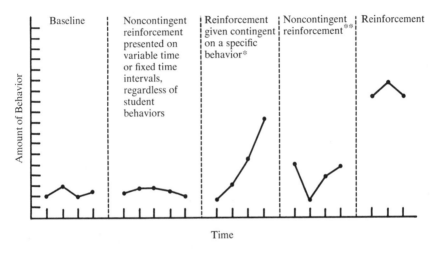

Time

* Reinforcement in this condition should be equal to or less than the amount of noncontingent reinforcement presented in the noncontingent component.

** The amount of noncontingent reinforcement in this condition should equal the amount given in the preceding contingent phase.

FIGURE 5–6. Prototype of the Noncontingent Reinforcement Analysis Design

Applied Example

Baer and Wolf (1970) reported an increase in cooperative play among preschool children. The teachers first collected

> baselines of cooperative and other related behaviors of the child, and of their own interaction with the child. Ten days of observation indicated that the child spent about 50 percent of each day in proximity with other children (meaning within 3 feet of them indoors, or 6 feet outdoors). Despite this frequent proximity, however, the child spent only about 2 percent of her day in cooperative play

with these children. The teachers, it was found, interacted with this girl about 20 percent of the day, not all of it pleasant. The teachers, therefore, set up a period of intense social reinforcement, offered not for cooperative play but free of any response requirement at all: the teachers took turns standing near the girl, attending closely to her activities, offering her materials, and smiling and laughing with her in a happy and admiring manner. The results of 7 days of this non-contingent extravagance of social reinforcement were straightforward: the child's cooperative play changed not at all, despite the fact that the other children of the group were greatly attracted to the scene, offering the child nearly double the chance to interact with them cooperatively. These 7 days having produced no useful change, the teachers then began their planned reinforcement of cooperative behavior. They defined cooperative behavior in four easily observed categories, subdivided into nine classes of very specific activities, with which a team of observers achieved reliabilities of 92 percent and better. Contingent social reinforcement, used in amounts less than half that given during the non-contingent period, increased the child's cooperative play from its usual 2 percent to a high of 40 percent in the course of 12 days of reinforcement. At that point, in the interests of certainty, the teachers discontinued contingent reinforcement in favor of non-contingent. In the course of 4 days, they lost virtually all of the cooperative behavior they had gained during the reinforcement period of the study, the child showing about a 5 percent average of cooperative play over that period of time. Naturally, the study concluded with a return to the contingent use of social reinforcement, a recovery of desirable levels of cooperative play, and a gradual reduction of the teacher's role in maintaining that behavior. (Baer and Wolf 1970, pp. 14–15)

These data appear in figure 5–7.

Application of Contingent Reinforcement to a Polar Behavior of a
Previously Reinforced Behavior as a Control Factor

Up–down, hot–cold, rough–smooth, day–night are examples of polar concepts in education. Polar behavior, as used here, refers to such sets of behaviors as in seat–out of seat, writing *was* for *saw,* talking–non-talking, hand up–hand down. To apply reinforcement of a polar behavior as a control procedure use the following steps:

1. Establish baseline on the target behavior (e.g. number of times students raise their hands to be called on to answer teacher's questions).
2. Reinforce the target behavior (e.g. hand raising).

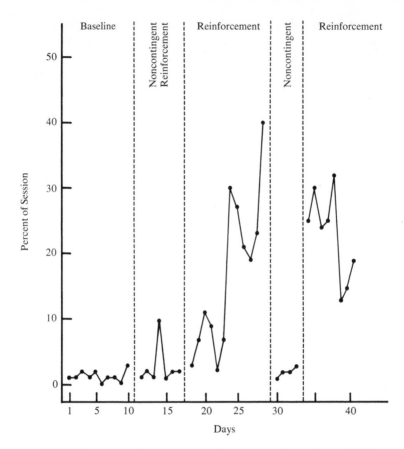

FIGURE 5–7.   *Percent of Session that a Pre-school Child Engaged in Cooperative and Other Related Behaviors. Example of a Reversal Design Analysis with Noncontingent Reinforcement (Adapted from Baer and Wolf 1970)*

3. Discontinue reinforcement of the target behavior and apply the reinforcement contingency to a polar behavior (e.g. hands down).
4. Return to reinforcement of the target behavior (e.g. hand raising) and discontinue reinforcement of the polar behavior.

Baer, Wolf, and Risley (1968) defined analysis as "a believable demonstration of the events that can be responsible for the occurrence or non-occurrence of that behavior." Reinforcement of a polar behavior is an appropriate analysis tactic when specific behaviors continue to persist after the teaching procedure is withdrawn. With this tactic the teacher may demonstrate that she can exercise control over events that increase the probability of the occurrence or nonoccurrence of that behavior. Figure 5–8 is a prototype of the reinforcement of a polar behavior design.

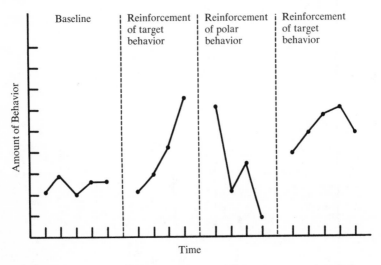

FIGURE 5–8.   *Prototype of the Reinforcement of a Polar Behavior Design*

Applied Example

An eleven-year-old student enrolled in a learning disability classroom persisted in reversing double numbers (e.g. 21 for 12; 31 for 13; 41 for 14). An example of his classroom work is presented in figure 1–1, part one, p. 9 of this book.

Baseline.   The teacher selected five number reversals which the student presently reversed. Each of the five numbers was printed on five separate four-by-five-inch note cards, making twenty-five response cards. An additional fifteen cards were printed. On each of the additional fifteen cards was one number, word, or letter that the student did not reverse. A total of forty response cards were used in obtaining baseline data. The five reversed numbers which were selected for training were: 13, 15, 17, 18, and 19.

During training the teacher and student were alone in a small tutor room. The teacher sat at a table facing the student. Prior to the session, the teacher shuffled the forty response cards to derive a random ordering.

To initiate the session, a pencil and an eight-by-eleven-inch piece of ruled paper were given the subject. After pencil and paper were given the student, the teacher looked at the response cards in sequence and asked the student to write the word, number, or letter that was indicated. At no time did the student see the writing on the cards. For example, the teacher looked at the first card and said, "Write the number 13." Then the teacher laid the card face down on the table and proceeded in identical manner with the remaining cards. No praise for correct responses or instruction for reversed responses was given during baseline.

Model and Reinforcement. Model and reinforcement condition was the same as baseline with two exceptions. First, whenever the student wrote 31 for 13 or 81 for 18, the teacher placed the corresponding note card of the correct model of the reversed number in front of the student and asked him to write the number again next to his reversed number. The next word, number, or letter in the random sequence was given following the student's response to the model. Second, for each 13 or 18 response that the student wrote correctly, *without a visual model setting the occasion for the response,* the teacher colored one rectangle of a series of fifteen small (approximately ¼-by-½-inch) vertical rectangles. When the rectangle series was completely colored the student was given a baseball (reinforcement). After meeting reinforcement criteria one time no other reinforcement was programmed for the study.

Polar Model. During this condition a polar model (i.e., 31 substituted for 13 or 81 substituted for 18) was presented. Whenever the student wrote 13 for 13 or 18 for 18, the teacher placed the corresponding polar note card in front of the student and asked him to write the number again. The next word, number or letter in the random sequence was given following the student's response to the polar model.

Follow-up. Follow-up was a return to the original baseline conditions on the seventh, fifteenth, and thirty-first days after termination of training.

Figure 5–9 gives a graphic presentation in percent of the student's correct responses to the numbers 13, 15, 17, 18, and 19 for the following conditions: baseline$_1$, model and reinforcement, baseline$_2$, model of a polar behavior, nonpolar model, and follow-up.

Baseline. During the first six days of baseline the student emitted almost no correct (nonreversed) responses to 13, 15, 17, 18, and 19. When the model and reinforcement condition was applied to the numbers 13 and 18, the student's correct responses to 13, 15, 17, 18, and 19 changed from zero in the last session of baseline$_1$ to 64 percent correct in the first session of model and reinforcement and 100 percent in the

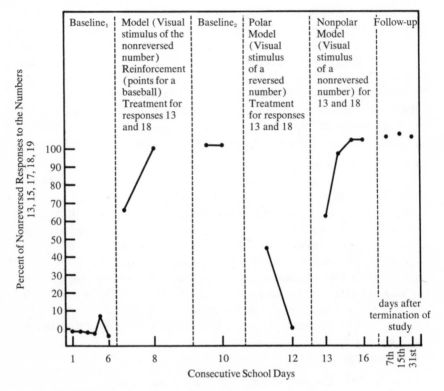

FIGURE 5–9.   Record of the Percent of Nonreversed Written Response to the Numbers 13, 15, 17, 18, 19 by an Eleven-year-old Student in a Learning Disability Classroom

second session. Following this behavior change the teacher removed the model and reinforcement contingencies and returned to baseline conditions to see if the behavior would approximate the previous baseline level. The student did not reverse his double numbers for two sessions in baseline₂. Each double number was written correctly 100 percent of the time. Since the student did not write number reversals in baseline₂, model of a polar behavior (e.g. 31 for 13) was presented whenever the student made a correct response of 13 or 18. Percent of nonreversed numbers decreased immediately following onset of the polar model contingency. All double numbers (13, 15, 17, 18, 19) were reversed in the second session of the polar model contingency.

When the nonpolar model was presented contingent on a reversed 13 or 18 response, correct number responses increased immediately. In the first session of this contingency, 65 percent of the student's double number responses were correct, 92 percent of the student's responses were correct in the second session, and all responses to 13, 15, 17, 18, and 19 were correct in the third and fourth sessions. The teacher terminated formal training on reversed double numbers at this point. However, follow-up post-checks were conducted to ascertain if the behavior change was being maintained. The behavior was checked with baseline conditions on 7, 15, and 31 days after termination of training. In each case 100 percent of the double number responses were correct. These data appear in figure 5–9.

Differential Reinforcement of Other Behaviors (DRO) as a Control Factor

The use of differential reinforcement of other behaviors in applied analysis is similar to the polar design. However, with differential reinforcement of other behaviors (DRO) any behavior except the target behavior may be reinforced. To apply the DRO analysis the following procedures must occur:

1. Establish baseline on the target behavior.
2. Reinforce the target behavior.
3. Differentially reinforce the occurrence of any behavior except the target behavior. In this condition, reinforcement is usually given on fixed or variable time schedules contingent on the non-occurrence of the target behavior. For example, if the target behavior were working on task, the teacher could at the end of each three minutes reinforce any behavior that was occurring except working on task.
4. Return to reinforcement of the target behavior.

Figure 5–10 is a prototype of the DRO design.

Applied Example

Reynolds and Risley (1968) reported a study designed to increase the frequency of talking of a four-year-old Negro girl. The girl exhibited an extremely low frequency of verbal behavior even after a normal adaptation of the pre-school setting and activities.

Baseline. During baseline, the percentage of ten-second intervals during which the student talked was recorded. The percentage of verbalizations during baseline averaged eleven percent during the first 129 days of school.

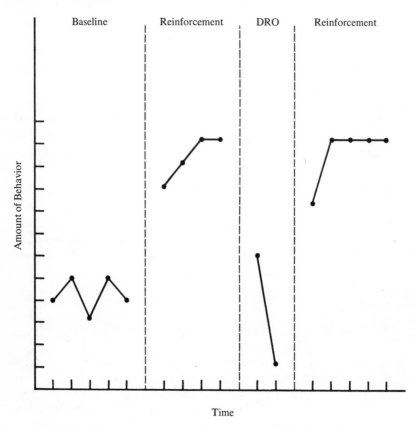

FIGURE 5–10.   *Prototype of the Differential Reinforcement of Other Behavior (DRO) Design*

Intervention.   To intervene Reynolds and Risley (1968) employed the
following conditions: (a) social interaction by the teachers was given
contingent upon student verbalizations; (b) whenever the student requested materials, access to them was contingent upon the student's
responding to teacher questions. The percentage of student verbalizations, during 73 days of the intervention condition, increased from an
average of eleven percent during baseline to seventy-five percent of the
ten-second intervals.

Differential Reinforcement of Other Behaviors.   The percentage of student verbalizations, during six days of DRO, decreased to an average of
six percent of the ten-second intervals.

Since the frequency of teacher attention was now higher, it
became necessary to investigate whether the increased instance
of teacher attention, per se, or the contingency of presenting

teacher attention was maintaining the verbal rate. It might be said that the child verbalized at a higher frequency simply because the teachers were attending and talking to her more, indicating that the higher incidence of teacher attention rather than its contingency of following the child's verbalizations was maintaining this frequency. Therefore, the teacher attention was maintained at as high a rate but was now made contingent upon non-verbalization by the child. Typically the teachers would attend to the child, praising her and providing her with materials while she was silently engaged in activities. For example, if the children near the child were asking for water and she picked up a cup, the teacher would reinforce the child's behavior of not asking by pouring water into her cup and keeping it filled as long as she was silent, and praising her for pouring from her cup, working hard, and keeping busy. Teachers removed their attention and the supplying source of materials for 15 to 30 seconds immediately following a verbalization by the child. (This procedure is often described as differential reinforcement of other behaviors, [DRO], since teacher attention is presented contingent upon any behavior except the behavior being measured, in this case talking.) (Reynolds and Risley 1968)

Intervention.   Teacher attention was again given contingent upon verbal responses of the student. The percentage of student verbalizations, during four days of this condition, increased to an average of fifty-one percent of the ten-second intervals. These data reported from the Reynolds and Risley (1968) study appear in figure 5–11.*

Parameters.   The reversal design with replications is the most powerful design in common use for analyzing effects of instruction. With this design, the baseline₂ condition serves as the control or predictor of what the behavior would have been had the teacher not intervened. For an example, see figure 5–12.

Unlike the A-B design, the reversal design will permit the teacher to account for causal factors in successful teaching methods. If, for example, behavior in baseline₂ approximates the recorded behavior in baseline₁ the teacher will have demonstrated an increase in probability that behavior change occurred because of her teaching technique. She can state with some assurance that it was her manipulation of instruction tactics that produced the change in student behavior.

While the reversal design can demonstrate causality and is the most powerful single organism design for analytic teaching, it has not received

---

* These data do not represent their complete study. ". . . further experimental analysis demonstrated that social interaction per se was not the reinforcer which maintained the increased verbalization; rather, for this child, the material reinforcers which accompanied the social interaction appeared to be the effective components of teacher attention" (Reynolds and Risley 1968).

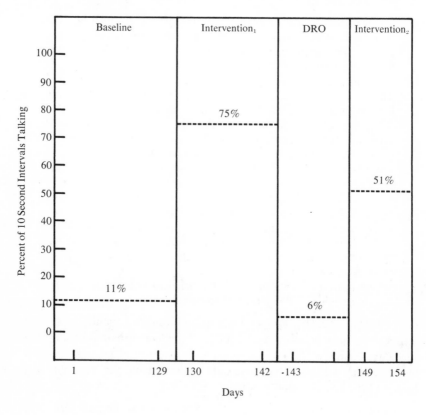

DRO—Teacher attention is presented contingent on any behavior except talking. Intervention[1 and 2]—Teachers' social attention contingent upon verbalization and student requests for materials granted contingent upon student verbal response to teachers' questions about those materials (adapted from data reported by Reynolds and Risley, 1968).

FIGURE 5–11.   The Average Percentage of 10-Second Intervals During which Talking Occurred

wide application in school settings. Perhaps there are three main reasons for the reluctance of school personnel to implement the reversal design. First, a major educational goal is to produce durable improvements in important behavior (e.g. reading, playing the piano, physical skills, etc.). Therefore, some behaviors once improved or acquisitioned may no longer be dependent on the instruction that created them. These socially significant behaviors may continue to persist after the teaching procedure is withdrawn unless a "motivational" variable is crucial. If the behavior change persists during baseline[2], no statements concerning effectiveness or causality can be made. This is the case with the A-B design since magnitude of the behavior change can be reported but no other state-

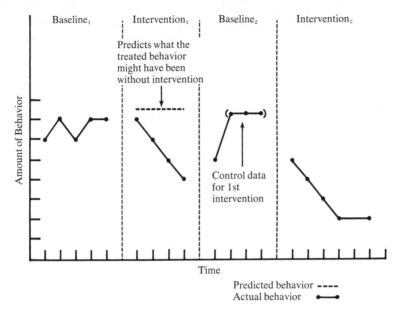

*FIGURE 5–12.   Example of the Function of the Reversal
Design*

ments can be made. The control data were lost since the behavior did
not reverse.

Second, reversals may not be desirable in some applied situations.
For example, the teacher may wish to select an evaluation design that
does not require a reversal if the target behavior is self-destructive,
physically harmful to others, or a less severe behavior that disrupts
instruction and the classroom.

Third, some may feel that it is immoral to employ an applied analysis
that sets the occasion for student behavior to be less desirable than
previously demonstrated. This is a legitimate concern of educators. Yet,
it should be kept in perspective that the reversal phase is of short duration (sometimes only three instruction sessions) and that desired
behavior is usually quickly reestablished during the intervention$_2$
condition.

Evaluation

You may choose to evaluate how well you comprehended the additional
information about analytic teaching by responding to the following test

items. Cover the answer column with a sheet of paper; then write your answers in the blank spaces provided. The correct answers may then be checked.

baseline
intervention
baseline$_2$
intervention$_2$

1. What are the four conditions in the reversal (ABAB) design?

   a.
   b.
   c.
   d.

only until a trend
   toward the terminal
   criteria is observed

2. How long should the first intervention in a reversal design be operative?

   a.

To demonstrate that in
   the absence of the
   intervention$_1$ procedure, behavior in
   baseline$_2$ will again
   approximate the
   magnitude of behav-
   ior recorded in
   baseline$_1$. A demon-
   stration of probable
   causality.

3. What is the purpose of the second baseline period?

   a.

noncontingent
   reinforcement
reinforcement of a po-
   lar behavior of a
   previously reinforced
   behavior
differential reinforce-
   ment of other
   behavior

4. What are the three variations on the reversal design?

   a.
   b.
   c.

Noncontingent
   reinforcement

5. _____ _____ is an excellent design if the intervention is the contingent application of social stimuli.

examples: up–down
           big–little
           in front of–
           behind

6. List one example of a polar concept (abstraction).

   a.

examples: writing *b*
for *d*
talking–
non-talking
in seat–out
of seat

7. Give one example of a polar behavior.

a.

teaching procedure

8. Reinforcement of a polar behavior is an appropriate analysis tactic when specific behaviors continue to persist after the _____ _____ is withdrawn.

differential reinforce-
ment of other
behavior

9. With _____ _____ _____ _____ _____ (DRO) analysis any behavior except the target behavior may be reinforced.

reversal design

10. The _____ _____ with replications is the most powerful design in common use for analyzing effects of instruction.

control

11. Baseline$_2$ condition in the reversal design serves as the _____ or predictor of what the behavior would have been had the teacher not intervened.

causal

12. Unlike the A-B design, the reversal design will permit the teacher to account for _____ factors in successful teaching methods.

some behaviors once
improved or acquisi-
tioned may no longer
be dependent on the
instruction that cre-
ated them
reversals may not be
desirable in some ap-
plied situations
some may feel that it is
immoral to employ
an applied analysis
that sets the occasion
for student behavior
to be less desirable
than previously dem-
onstrated

13. What are three possible reasons why the reversal design has not received wide application in school settings?

a.

b.

c.

Exercise 5–2

Graph a hypothetical example of a reversal design.

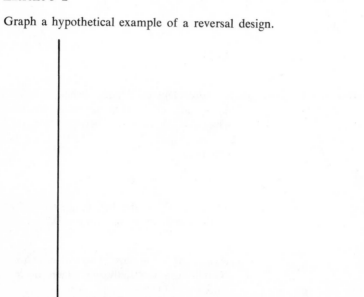

Multiple Baseline Designs

On some occasions, the reversal design can present problems for teachers. For example, many school behaviors do not reverse in the second baseline condition, other responses such as aggressive behavior, may be undesirable for reversal, and some teachers may object to any reversal conditions. When these problems are evident, the multiple baseline design can be employed since the logic of this design does not call for a reversal condition.

The multiple baseline design may be applied in three ways:

1. two or more different but similar *behaviors* of a given individual or group;
2. *one behavior* of a given individual or group that occurs in at least *two different environmental conditions;*
3. same behavior of two or more *different individuals* or *groups.*

Two or More Different but Similar Behaviors of a
Given Individual or Group

Condition A: Two or more different behaviors of a given individual are measured at the same time before intervention (baseline for all behaviors).

Condition B: The intervention (teaching) tactic is *implemented on only one behavior* following baselines. Measurement is maintained for the other behaviors which remain in baseline status. After a behavior change is generated for the first intervention, the same teaching procedure is applied to the second behavior. Following behavior change of the first and second behavior, the intervention tactic is applied to the third behavior, and so on.

Figure 5–13 provides a graphic prototype of the multiple baseline design employing two or more different but similar behaviors of a given individual or group.

Applied Example

STUDENT

The student was a nonverbal, severely retarded five-year-old boy who attended a preschool for trainable mentally retarded children at the Mental Retardation Training Program, The Ohio State University. He had a history of food rejection and rumination. Prior to this study the student was hospitalized for malnutrition.

PRE-BASELINE—PINPOINTING THE TARGET BEHAVIORS

Three successive 15-minute observation periods were employed to assess the student's eating behavior before compiling formal baseline records. These observations indicated that the student could manipulate a spoon. However, enticing him to open his mouth and swallow entailed constant attention, priming, and reward (i.e., preferred foods such as pudding were given contingent on eating nonpreferred foods) from the teacher. From these pre-baseline data, "self-feeding" was selected as the target behavior. The setting for baseline assessment of "self-feeding" behaviors included the student and teacher sitting alone at a small table during the noon meal. A glass of juice, plate of food, and spoon was located directly in front of the student. Through the meal the teacher ignoring all student behavior. Measurement consisted of the number of spoonfuls of food that the student swallowed. When this procedure was initiated it was demonstrated that "self-feeding" was not a problem. However, observation did show that the student emitted multiple mealtime problem behaviors at high rates. The behaviors selected for deceleration were:

1. *Throwing* the glass, plate, food, or spoon on the floor.
2. *Hitting* the spoon on an object such as the table, chair or plate. Each burst or volley of hitting responses was recorded

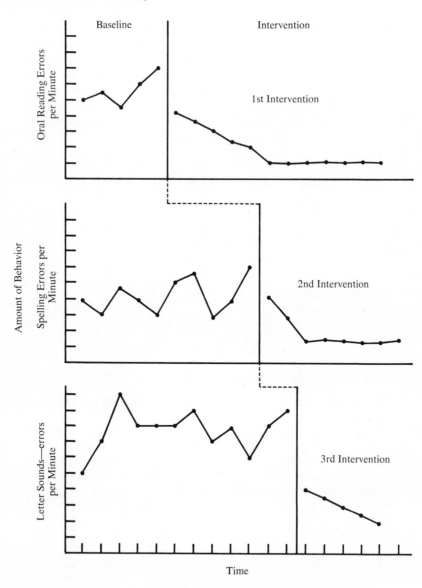

FIGURE 5–13.   *Prototype of the Multiple Baseline Design
—Two or More Behaviors, a Given Indi-
vidual or Group*

as one response, e.g., six rapid hits followed by a pause, then
10 more rapid hits would be recorded as two hitting responses.

3. *Spitting* food or saliva from mouth.

4. *Ruminating* or regurgitating previously swallowed food back to the mouth then returning the food back to the stomach. This response was characterized by a gargling sound in the throat accompanied by some movement of the neck muscles.

PROCEDURE—INTERVENTION I—
THROWING, HITTING, AND SPITTING

Intervention I reports the effects of a timeout technique on decelerating mealtime problem behaviors. A multiple-baseline research design (Baer, Wolf, and Risley 1968) demonstrated the function of the timeout variable.

Baseline: Frequency of throwing, hitting and spitting responses was recorded during the noon meal. The teacher and student sat at a small table in the clinic kitchen. A glass of juice, plate of food and spoon was located on the table directly in front of the student. The student's task during Period I was to eat his meal. The session duration was timed by the teacher with a stopwatch. Average duration of the meal was approximately 15 minutes per session with a range of 9 minutes and 38 seconds to 29 minutes and 10 seconds. Using a clipboard, pencil, and paper, the teacher tallied the frequency of throwing, hitting, and spitting responses that occurred during the meal. The teacher did not talk, touch, or attend to the behaviors of the student during Period I. Her task was simply to record the number of occurrences of throwing, hitting, and spitting. The session was terminated after the student ate all or most of the food on his plate.

Intervention Procedure: Following baseline data collection, a timeout procedure was programmed. During this procedure, the student's drink, food, and spoon was removed from the table for 1-minute immediately following each throwing or hitting response. Drink, food, and spoon was returned to the table after the 1-minute interval timed out. If, however, the student was emitting disruptive behaviors when the 1-minute timed out (e.g., temper tantrums, etc.) the drink, food, and spoon was not returned until the student was in his chair and exhibiting appropriate readiness. This procedure was applied sequentially. Initially, timeout was contingent on throwing responses while hitting responses maintained baseline status. Following four initial timeout sessions, the intervention procedure was concurrently applied to throwing and hitting responses.

Interobserver agreement: During two meals of the study, a second independent observer made simultaneous frequency counts of the target behaviors with the teacher. Percentage of observer agreement was computed from two records.

RESULTS

Interobserver agreement was recorded twice during baseline for each target behavior. Interobserver agreement for throwing was 90% and 100%; hitting, 100% and 83%; and spitting, 33% and 71%.

The frequency count for each target behavior per session was converted to rate of response (rate $= \dfrac{\text{frequency of occurrence}}{\text{duration of session}}$). A rate measure rather than frequency count was employed because session time was not constant through the study.

Figure 5–14 represents the rate of occurrence of throwing, hitting and spitting during mealtime. The rate measure was rounded to the nearest whole number if responses were greater than one per minute or to the nearest tenth if less than one occurrence per minute. For example, 1.3 responses per minute was recorded as 1.0; 1.5 as 2.0. Likewise, .16 was recorded as .2; .12 as .1. The successive timeout conditions are indicated in Figure 5–14 by vertical lines. Timeout was introduced on the sixth session for throwing behavior and on the eleventh session for hitting. Horizontal arrows in Figure 5–14 indicate the duration of each condition. Data reported in Figure 5–14 demonstrate that timeout systematically decelerated the manipulated behavior. For example, the mean rate of throwing was .8 responses per minute during baseline but dropped to a mean rate of .1 responses per minute during the timeout condition. The mean hitting responses during baseline was .5 per minute. During timeout, hitting responses decelerated to a mean of .1 per minute. Timeout was not programmed for spitting because this behavior decelerated to zero occurrences without intervention after timeout was applied to throwing and hitting responses. (Cooper, Jacobsen, Payne 1971)

One Behavior, of a Given Individual or Group, that Occurs in at Least Two Different Environmental Conditions or Locations

Condition A: One behavioral pinpoint of one individual or group is measured in different environmental conditions (e.g. home-school; lunch room-play ground; reading class-music activity; morning-afternoon; etc.) to generate baseline data for each location.

Condition B: The intervention (teaching) tactic is implemented on the one behavior in only one location following baselines. The behavioral occurrences in other locations are continuously measured and maintained in baseline status. After a behavior change is generated in the first location, the same teaching procedure is applied in the second

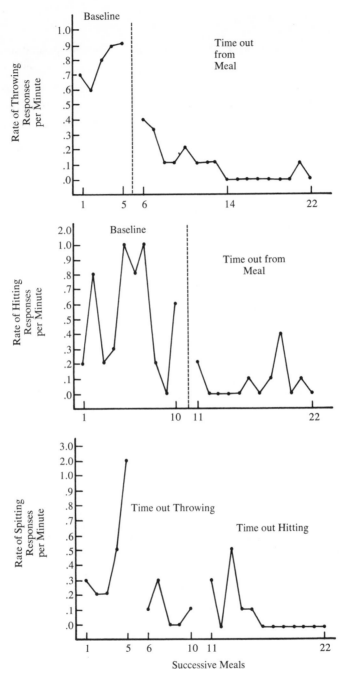

FIGURE 5–14. Concurrent Rates of Throwing, Hitting, and Spitting Responses, through Baseline and Intervention Procedures of the Study

location. Following behavior change in the first and second location, the intervention tactic is applied in the third location, and so on.

Figure 5–15 provides a graphic prototype of the multiple baseline design employing one behavior of a given individual or group that occurs in at least two different environmental locations.

Applied Example

This applied example (one behavior, a given individual or group, two or more different environmental conditions or locations) is a continuation of the Cooper et al. (1971) study that illustrated different but similar behaviors of a given individual.

SUBJECT

The subject was nonverbal, severely retarded five-year old boy who attended a pre-school for trainable mentally retarded children at the Mental Retardation Training Program, The Ohio State University. He had a history of food rejection and rumination. Prior to this study the student was hospitalized for malnutrition.

PROCEDURE—INTERVENTION II—RUMINATING

Intervention II reports the effects of different procedures for decelerating rumination. A combination of a reversal and multiple-baseline research design (Baer, Wolf and Risley 1968) demonstrated the function of the intervention variables.

BASELINE

Rate of rumination was recorded by the teacher during three successive time periods: (1) during mealtime in the clinic kitchen in which duration of the session varied, (2) during the five minutes immediately following mealtime in the clinic kitchen, and (3) during a subsequent 5-minute period in a pre-school activity room.

Period I. Frequency of ruminating response were recorded during the noon meal. The teacher and student sat at a small table in the clinic kitchen. A glass of juice, plate of food and spoon were located on the table directly in front of the student. The student's task during Period I was to eat his meal. The session duration was timed by the teacher with a stopwatch. Average duration of the meal was approximately 15 minutes per session. Using a clipboard, pencil, and paper, the teacher tallied the frequency of ruminating responses that occurred during the meal. The teacher did not talk, touch, or attend to the behaviors of the student during Period I.

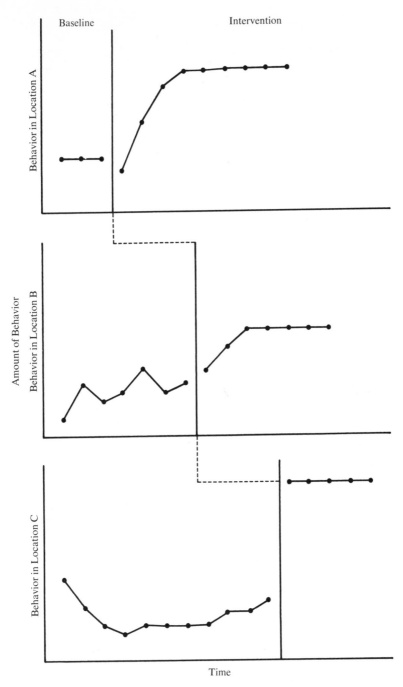

FIGURE 5–15. *Prototype of the Multiple Baseline Design, One Behavior, a Given Individual or Group, Two or More Different Conditions*

Her task was simply to record the number of occurrences of rumination. The session was terminated after the student ate all or most of the food on his plate.

Period II. Frequency of ruminating responses was recorded for a duration of 5 minutes immediately following the meal in the clinic kitchen. Student behaviors during Period II were unstructured. For example, the student could sit at the table, walk, explore cupboard space, or what not. To initiate Period II, the teacher set a small timer (Foxx and Martin 1971) for five minutes. The teacher's responsibilities during Period II included cleaning the table and dishes, and recording the number of ruminating responses emitted by the student. The teacher used a wrist digital counter (Lindsley 1968) to record the number of ruminating responses. A signal from the timer indicated a time lapse of five minutes and termination of the recording session. Following termination of Period II, the teacher accompanied the student to a pre-school activity classroom located adjacent to the clinic kitchen.

Period III. Frequency of ruminating responses was recorded during the first five minutes of free play in an activity room. Observation in the free-play setting was initiated following teacher/student entrance to the classroom. Session duration was timed in Period III, as in Period II, with a small timer (Foxx and Martin 1971). Student behavior was unstructured during the free-play period. The student played with activity materials (toys, slide, jungle jim, etc.) and interacted with the teacher. Teacher behaviors included playing games and showing affection (smiling, hugging and patting) to the student. Also, the teacher recorded the occurrence of ruminations by activating a wrist counter (Lindsley 1968).

Intervention Procedures: Intervention Procedure *A* was applied following baseline data collection. Contingent on the occurrence of a ruminating response, the teacher immediately placed her cupped hand firmly over the student's mouth and concurrently voiced an emphatic "no." The teacher's hand was over the student's mouth for a duration of approximately one second. Following this, the teacher stopped all social interaction (i.e., play, talking, patting, etc.) with the student for 30 seconds. The teacher ignored all ruminating responses that occurred during the 30-second timeout conditions. This first intervention was applied only in Period III (freeplay) with Periods I and II maintaining in baseline status.

Intervention Procedure *B* was the same as the Intervention *A* except that the teacher did not employ the 30-second timeout period. That is, the second procedure consisted only of the teacher immediately placing her cupped hand firmly over the student's mouth and concurrently voicing an emphatic "no" contingent on *each* ruminating response. Intervention procedure *B* was applied sequentially—first to Period III (free-play) with Periods II and I maintained in baseline status, then to Periods III and II (free-play and first five minutes after mealtime) with Period I maintained in baseline condition, and finally to Periods III, II and I (free-play, first five minutes after mealtime, and during the meal).

Interobserver Agreement: A second independent observer and the teacher made simultaneous frequency counts of ruminating responses in Periods I, II, and III during baseline and each intervention condition of the study. Percentage of observer agreement was computed from the two records. Five interobserver recordings were made in Periods I and II and seven in Period III.

RESULTS

Interobserver agreement of ruminating responses was recorded in each condition of the study. Out of a total of 17 checks, nine interobserver recordings attained 100% agreement, three were 90% or above, and two were above 85% but less than 90% agreement. Agreement between the remaining three checks was very low. However, in actuality the difference in tabulation was only one response in each check. For example, the teacher recorded the occurrence of one ruminating response while the independent observer recorded two responses during one check. With another check, the teacher recorded three responses while the observer reported two occurrences. And once again, the teacher recorded the occurrence of two responses while the observer recorded one.

The frequency count for ruminations per session was converted to rate of response (rate $= \dfrac{\text{frequency of occurrence}}{\text{duration of session}}$). A rate measure rather than frequency count was employed because session time of Period I was not constant through the study.

Figure 5–16 represents the rate of occurrence of rumination during Period III (free-play), Period II (five minutes immediately following mealtime) and Period I (mealtime). The rate measure was rounded to the nearest whole number if responses were greater than one per minute or to the nearest tenth if less than one occurrence per minute. For example, 1.3 responses per minute was recorded as 1.0, 1.5 as 2.0. Likewise, .16 was recorded as .2; .12 as .1. The intervention conditions are indicated in figure 5–16 by vertical lines. Intervention *B* was successively programmed on the 17th session in Period III, on the 20th session in Period II, and on the 24th session in Period I. Each period was simultaneously returned to baseline condition from the 27th through the 28th session. Intervention *B* was reinstated for all periods on the 29th session. Data reported in figure 5–16 demonstrate that Intervention *A* (hand cupped over mouth, teacher response "no," and 30-second timeout from teacher attention) was ineffective in decelerating ru-

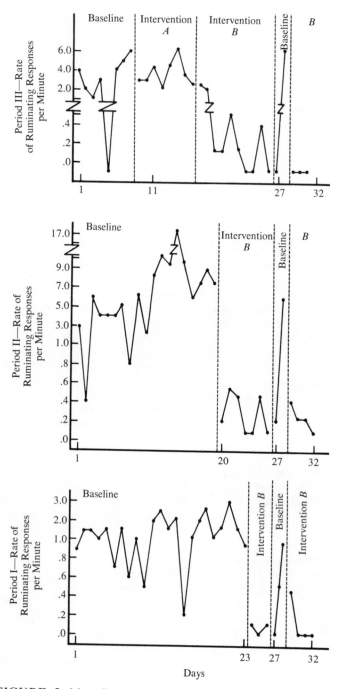

FIGURE 5–16. Concurrent Rates of Ruminating Responses during Period III, Period II, and Period I, through Baseline, Intervention A and Intervention B

minating responses that occurred in Period III. The mean rate of ruminating responses was 3.0 responses per minute for both baseline and Intervention *A*. However, the data reported in figure 5–16 demonstrates that Intervention *B* (same as *A* but without timeout) systematically decelerated the occurrence of rumination. For example, the mean rate of response occurring in baseline and Intervention *A* during Period III was 3.0 per minute but dropped to a mean of .5 during Intervention *B*. The mean rate of ruminating responses during baseline of Period II was 6.0 per minute. During Intervention *B*, ruminating responses decelerated to .2 per minute. For Period I, the mean rate of response during baseline was 2.0 per minute but dropped to .1 during Intervention *B*. Baseline conditions were reinstated in all time periods following the sequential application of Intervention *B*. In this second baseline condition, rate of ruminating responses accelerated from zero occurrences to 5.0 per minute in Period III; from a rate of .2 to 5.0 in Period II; and from zero to a rate of .9 per minute in Period I. The reinstatement of Intervention *B* again decelerated the rate of ruminating responses in each time period.

Same Behavior of Two or More Different Individuals or Groups

Condition A: A behavior of two or more individuals or groups is measured prior to intervention (baseline for each individual or group).

Condition B: The intervention tactic is applied to *only one individual* following baseline. The pinpointed behavior of the other individual is continuously measured and maintained in baseline status. After a behavior change is generated for the first individual, the same teaching tactic is applied to the second person. Following behavior change of the first and second individuals, the intervention tactic is applied to the third person, and so on.

Figure 5–17 provides a graphic prototype of the multiple baseline design employing the same behavior of two or more different individuals or groups.

Applied Example

The Stanberry and Harris (1971) study illustrates the use of the multiple baseline design with the same behavior for three groups.

Population and setting: Eighteen seventh, eighth, and ninth grade pupils who attended a suburban junior high of 1,130 students were selected as subjects because they had the highest rate of being tardy

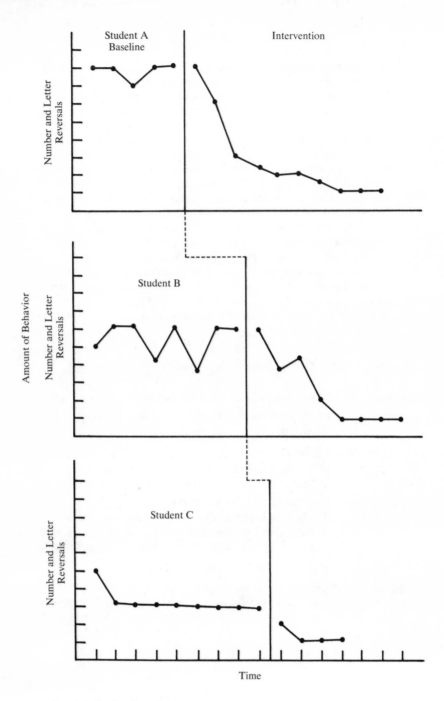

FIGURE 5–17.   Prototype of the Multiple Baseline Design,
Same Behavior, Two or More Individuals
or Groups

to one or more of their six daily classes. The mean number of tardies for each of these pupils over a five-day period prior to the experiment was found to be 0.9, or just less than one per day. The eighteen students were randomly assigned to one of three groups of six pupils.

Behavior measured: Tardiness was defined as not being across the threshold of the doorway when the tardy bell rang. The teachers of the students were given forms on which to record whether or not these pupils were tardy. Each teacher selected a reliable student who was punctual as a second observer. The records of the teachers and the pupils were compared. Agreement in their records was computed by dividing the smaller record by the larger and multiplying by 100. Agreement ranged from 83% to 96%.

Experimental procedures and results: Baseline: Prior to any manipulation, baseline records of the number of tardies were made for each of the three groups. Baseline for Group I lasted five days, for Group II ten days, for Group III 13 days. The mean baseline rate of tardiness for Group I was 8.4, for Group II 7.9, for Group III 5.8. Signing In and Points for Promptness: Beginning at successive intervals (Group I—6th day, Group II—11th day, Group III—14th day) the pupils were called together by the assistant principal and were given a form for their teachers to sign and to indicate whether they were on time or late to class. They were told this was a new approach to solving their tardiness problem and that they would receive five points each time they were on time. They were told their goal should be to accumulate 165 points. (In order to reach this goal they could be tardy no more than two times per week.) It was hoped that reaching this goal would prove reinforcing and no other back-ups were offered for the points. Under these conditions the mean rates of tardiness were, Group I 3.8, Group II 1.2, Group III 2.4.

Discussion: This study showed that the procedure of having pupils sign in with teachers and of giving students points for being prompt was effective in reducing tardiness. A multiple-baseline design provided scientific verification but would have been strengthened considerably if recording had been continued with Groups I and II through the full 18 days of the experiment. It is uncertain whether tardiness was reduced because signing in when tardy was punishing or whether earning points for being on time was reinforcing. (Stanberry and Harris 1971)

Directive teachers use the following steps when employing a multiple baseline design.

1. *Assess* social and academic skills.
2. *Pinpoint* and *define* the behavior to be modified.
3. Specify the *terminal behavior*.

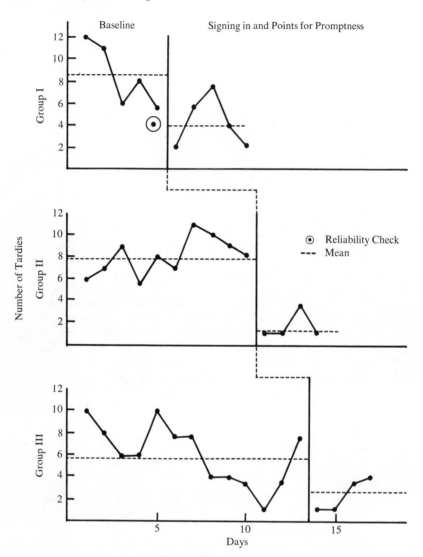

FIGURE 5–18. *A Record of the Number of Tardies by Three Groups of Six Pupils in a Junior High School*

4. Select an appropriate *measurement tactic*.
5. *Measure* the occurrence or nonoccurrence of:
   a. one or more target behaviors of a given individual or group;
   b. one behavior, of a given individual, that occurs in at least two different environmental locations;
   c. same behavior of two or more different individuals or groups.

6. Sequentially apply the intervention strategy to:
   a. two or more target behaviors;
   b. different environmental locations;
   c. two or more different individuals or groups.
7. Discontinue instruction after:
   a. the two or more target behaviors have reached terminal criteria;
   b. the target behavior has reached terminal criteria in each environmental location;
   c. the two or more different individuals or groups have all reached terminal criteria.
8. Following the formal termination of instruction, occasionally measure the pinpointed behavior or behaviors to see if the skill is still approximating the terminal criteria.

The major advantage of the multiple baseline strategy is the elimination of the "undesirable" aspects of the reversal design (e.g. target behavior is dangerous or self-destructive, unwillingness of some teachers to employ reversals in teaching, etc.). As with the reversal design, the multiple baseline design will permit the teacher to account for causal factors in successful teaching methods. In the multiple baseline design, the second behavior, second condition, or second individual serves as the control or predictor to increase the probability that coincidence was not responsible for the first behavior change. For example, see figure 5-19.

The application of the same intervention procedure to the second behavior, condition, or individual may further increase confidence that the treatment variable was the factor responsible for behavior change. A multiple baseline analysis employing two baselines can provide strong implications concerning effectiveness of the intervention technique. However, the greater the number of baselines used in analysis the greater the confidence that a functional relationship has been demonstrated. The question is, "How many times must the intervention tactic be applied, with a corresponding behavior change, before it is convincing that the intervention tactic generated the behavior change?" Usually three or four baselines will produce almost completely convincing results.

One consideration in using the multiple baseline design is the induction effect. Induction effect occurs when the intervention tactic is applied to one behavior and affects not only the treated behavior, but the other baselines as well. It may be a low probability that induction will occur using baselines from two or more given individuals. A higher probability may exist when using only one subject.

When induction occurs, control information from the nontreated baselines is lost. In such cases, the multiple baseline design becomes, in reality, an A-B design. The teacher can only establish whether or not the

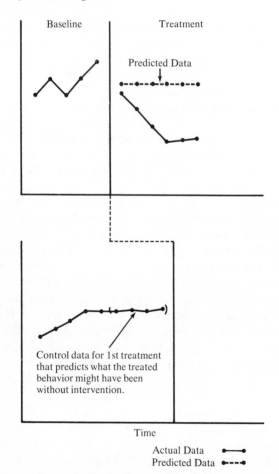

FIGURE 5-19. *Example of the Function of the Multiple Baseline Design*

students' behavior changed and the degree to which it changed. No statements of causality can be made. However, an alternative is available during induction if the teacher wishes to demonstrate causality or effective teaching. When this occurs, the teacher should simply change from a multiple baseline design to a reversal design (ABAB).

After the induction effect, return to baseline condition. If the behavior then approximates the recorded behavior prior to treatment, a demonstration of causality is at hand. Following the return to baseline, treatment should be reinstated.

Some key points should be followed in using a multiple baseline design. *First,* when using baseline of two or more different behaviors of a given individual or group, the *behaviors* should be *similar*. For example, verbal spelling errors would probably make a more convincing control baseline for oral reading errors than, say, out of seat behavior. The closer the similarity among baselines, the more acceptable is the control data.

Second, data for all *baselines* are collected in close *temporal proximity* (e.g. all baselines are started on the same day).

Evaluation

You may choose to evaluate how well you comprehended the information about multiple baselines by responding to the following test items. Cover the answer column with a sheet of paper; then write your answers in the blank spaces provided. The correct answers may then be checked.

two or more different but similar behaviors of a given individual or group one behavior, of a given individual or group, that occurs in at least two different environmental conditions some behavior of two or more different individuals or groups	1. List three procedural applications of the multiple baseline design. a. b. c.
causal	2. As with the reversal design, the multiple baseline design will permit the teacher to account for _____ factors in successful teaching methods.
control	3. In the multiple baseline design, the second behavior, second condition, or second individual serves as the _____ or predictor to increase the probability that coincidence was not responsible for the first behavior change.
baselines	4. The greater the number of _____ used in the multiple baseline analysis, the greater the confidence that a functional relationship has been demonstrated.

induction

5. One consideration in using the multiple baseline design is the _____ effect.

control

6. When induction occurs _____ information from the nontreated baselines is lost.

Exercise 5–4

Graph a hypothetical example of a multiple baseline design.

Summary

Part three has been concerned with designs sufficient for analytic teaching. Analytic teaching is the educational process of demonstrating what student behavior is emitted in both the presence and absence of the teacher's instruction procedures. The following designs were presented:

1. The A–B design with two conditions
   a. Pretest or baseline period (measurement) before intervention
   b. Measurement during the intervention or instruction strategy

2. The reversal design (ABAB) with four conditions
   a. Pretest or baseline period (measurement) before intervention
   b. Measurement during the intervention or instruction strategy
   c. Return to baseline conditions
   d. Reinstate instruction strategy

3. Variations on the reversal design
   a. The application of noncontingent reinforcement as a control condition
   b. The application of contingent reinforcement to a polar behavior of a previously reinforced behavior as a control condition
   c. Differential reinforcement of other behavior as a control condition

4. The multiple baseline design applied in three ways
   a. Two or more different but similar behaviors of a given individual or group
   b. One behavior, of a given individual or group, that occurs in at least two different environmental conditions
   c. Same behavior of two or more different individuals or groups

Exercise 5–5

You should now be ready to conduct a complete behavioral analysis. The following outline will be helpful in guiding you through your first projects. Reference is made to sources for the reader to review or use. Each reference is coded and can be found under the section entitled "sources." Following the outline is a model of a behavioral analysis for your study.

To be completed by the participant:

Your name _____

Your position _____

Address _____

Phone _____

This program is designed for (circle one):
  1. Training teachers
  2. Training parents
  3. Training children

Date Program was prepared: _____

Checked and approved (do not complete)

  By _____

  Date _____

A. *Initial Specifications*

  Step 1: Name the behavior or behaviors you want to increase or decrease.

  _____

  Step 2: Give your definition of the behavior. Include only definitions that generate independent observer agreements of 80% or higher.

  _____

  Step 3: Describe the characteristics of the population to be served; e.g. sex, age, grade, education, school success, employment, etc.

  _____

  _____

Step 4: Indicate how the population will be selected; e.g. random selection, assigned by teacher, selected through assessments or criteria levels, volunteers, etc.

_____

Step 5: How many students (parents, teachers) will be selected?

_____

B. *Measurable Objectives*

Step 1: Specify objectives.
These objectives must be:
a) Specific
b) Measurable
c) Functional (useful to those you are treating or teaching)

Write your objectives below: (Source: 3)

1. _____

2. _____

3. _____

4. _____

5. _____

Step 2: Indicate terminal behavior
a) Describe the conditions under which the learned responses will occur.
b) Indicate exactly what the learners will be doing so as to demonstrate their newly acquired behavior.
c) Describe how *well* the learner must perform the task; i.e. specify terminal behavior.
d) Be specific.
e) Relate the terminal behavior to each objective.

Write your terminal behavior below. Follow the same sequence as in Step 1. (Source: 3)

1. _____

2. _____

3. _____

4. _____

5. _____

C. *Baseline Data Collection* (Source: 7, Part I)

    Step 1: Describe measurement technique. These descriptions should be described in enough detail so that another person could replicate your measurement tactics after reading your descriptions. You may choose to employ more than one measurement technique for your study. Choose the techniques you used from the list below and elaborate.

        a) Direct measurement of permanent products (e.g. written responses) _____

        _____

        b) Observational recording
        Event recording (e.g. frequency of occurrence, tally, etc.) _____

        _____

        Duration recording (e.g. amount of time engaged in a behavior) _____

        _____

        Interval recording (e.g. the occurrence or nonoccurrence of a behavior within a specified interval of time)

        _____

        _____

        Time sample (e.g. the occurrence or nonoccurrence of a behavior immediately following a specified interval of time) _____

        _____

Step 2: Describe materials used in data collection: e.g. stopwatch, worksheets, etc. If you use a checklist or special forms, attach them to this form. _____

_____

Step 3: Describe reliability measures (interobserver agreement). Attach instructions that are given to the independent observers. _____

_____

Step 4: Will you group your data (mean, mode, median) or make entirely separate graphs for each student (parent, teacher)?

_____

_____

Step 5: Graph your data on the attached forms.

D. *Procedures*

Step 1: Indicate the procedures you will use to achieve the objectives stated under B.

a) What independent variable (treatment) will be used to produce behavior change; e.g. reinforcement, curriculum material changes, social models and imitation, etc.?

_____

_____

b) What are the contingency criteria for delivery of treatment; e.g. continuous, fixed time intervals, variable time intervals, fixed number (ratio) of responses, variable number (ratio) of responses? _____

_____

_____

c) If you are using reinforcers or other consequences that must follow the behavior but which cannot be delivered immediately, how will you bridge this time delay?

_____

_____

d) If others are delivering treatment (e.g. parents or teachers) how will you know that it has been delivered?

_____

_____

Describe the procedures you will follow: (Sources: 1, 2, 4, 6, 7, Parts II, III)

1. _____

_____

2. _____

_____

3. _____

_____

4. _____

_____

5. _____

_____

6. _____

_____

7. _____

_____

8. _____

_____

9. _____

_____

10. _____

_____

E. *Applied Behavior Analysis* (Source: 7, Part I)

The Reversal Design

1. Baseline$_1$—Record of ongoing behavior prior to intervention (Step 3).
2. Intervention procedure—Introduction of Step 4.
3. Baseline$_2$—Withdraw intervention procedures and return to Baseline$_1$ conditions.
4. Intervention procedure$_2$—Reinstate the intervention procedures (same as intervention procedure$_1$).
5. Post-checks.

The Multiple Baseline Design

A multiple baseline analysis can be used when two or more similar behaviors are emitted by the same subject, when the same behavior occurs in different stimulus conditions, or when the same behavior occurs in more than one subject. When these conditions exist, contingencies may be applied to one behavior then the other, in one stimulus condition then the next, or with one subject then sequentially with other subjects. Functional relationships are established if changes in each behavior correspond to experimental manipulations.

a) Select the design you will follow in order to evaluate the effects of your instruction. Indicate the design you have chosen below:

_____

b) Define the criteria used for changing conditions (e.g. fixed time for each, criterion levels, "stability," etc.)

_____

_____

_____

c) Label and define, on the graph, each condition you implement. These labels and definitions should be concise, but complete enough that others would know your tactics without making reference to your text.

F. *Abstract*

Population and Setting:

Target Behavior and Interobserver Agreement:

Treatment and Result:

Summary Statement:

Sources

1. Stephens, Thomas M. *Directive Teaching of Children With Learning and Behavioral Handicaps.* Columbus, Ohio: Charles E. Merrill Publishing Co., 1970.

2. Homme, Lloyd and others. *How to Use Contingency Contracting in the Classroom.* Champaign, Ill.: Research Press, 1969.

3. Mager, Robert F. *Preparing Instructional Objectives.* Palo Alto, Calif.: Fearon Publishers, 1962.

4. Mager, Robert F. and Kenneth M. Beach, Jr. *Developing Vocational Instruction.* Palo Alto, Calif.: Fearon Publishers, 1967.

5. Mager, Robert F. *Developing Attitude Toward Learning.* Palo Alto, Calif.: Fearon Publishers, 1968.
6. Becker, Wesley C. *Parents Are Teachers.* Champaign, Ill.: Research Press, 1971.
7. Hall, R. Vance. *Managing Behavior, Parts I, II, III.* H & H Enterprises, Inc., 9001 West 65th Drive, Merriam, Kansas 66202, 1970.

To be completed by the participant:

Your name   Jack Priser

Your position   School Psychologist

Address   345 E. Mulberry Street, Lancaster, Ohio 43130

Phone _____

This program is designed for (circle one):

1. Training teachers
2. Training parents
3. Training children

Date Program was prepared: November 1, 1971

Checked and approved (do not complete)

By _____

Date _____

A. *Initial Specifications*

   Step 1: Name the behavior or behaviors you want to increase or decrease.

   Decrease the number of vocalizations emitted by a 2-year-old boy during a ten-minute segment (9:30–9:40 A.M.) of a language arts–social studies class.

   Step 2: Give your definition of the behavior. Include only definitions that generate independent observer agreements of 80% or higher.

   Vocalization—comments or audible vocal noises initiated by the student. Must occur without being called on by teacher. Must not be a response to another student's communication directed specifically to him. Each specific comment or audible vocalization counts as 1 vocalization. Any behavior which serves to indicate termination of a comment or noise will serve to separate the vocalizations; e.g. a breath, a time interval that breaks the rhythm of the emission, attending to another task, or a change in topic from one sentence to another, etc.

Step 3: Describe the characteristics of the population to be served; e.g. sex, age, grade, education, school success, employment, etc.

One 12-year-old boy repeating 6th grade. History of low academic achievement.

Step 4: Indicate how the population will be selected; e.g. random selection, assigned by teacher, selected through assessments or criteria levels, volunteers, etc.

Step 5: How many students (parents, teachers) will be selected?

B. *Measurable Objectives*

Step 1: Specify objectives
These objectives must be:
a) Specific
b) Measurable
c) Functional (useful to those you are treating or teaching)

Write your objectives below: (Source: 3)

1. To decrease the number of vocalizations emitted by a 12-year-old boy during a ten-minute segment (9:30–9:40 A.M.) of a language arts–social studies class.

Step 2: Indicate terminal behavior

a) Describe the conditions under which the learned responses will occur.
b) Indicate exactly what the learners will be doing so as to demonstrate their newly acquired behavior.
c) Describe how *well* the learner must perform the task; i.e. specify terminal behavior.
d) Be specific.
e) Relate the terminal behavior to each objective.

Write your terminal behavior below. Follow the same sequence as in Step 1. (Source: 3)

1. Given a ten-minute (9:30–9:30 A.M.) segment of a language arts or social studies class discussion or seatwork assignment, the student will emit 50% (or fewer) of the number of vocalizations emitted prior to the implementation of the treatment variable.

C. *Baseline Data Collection* (Sources: 7, Part I)

Step 1: Describe measurement technique. These descriptions should be described in enough detail so that another person could replicate your measurement tactics after reading your descriptions. You may choose to employ more than one measurement technique for your study. Choose the techniques you used from the list below and elaborate.

a) Direct measurement of permanent products (e.g. written responses)

_____

_____

b) Observational recording

Event recording (e.g. frequency of occurrence, tally, etc.)

During the ten-minute interval, the observer will tally the vocalizations as defined.

Duration recording (e.g. amount of time engaged in a behavior)

_____

_____

Interval recording (e.g. the occurrence or nonoccurrence of a behavior within a specified interval of time)

_____

_____

Time sample (e.g. the occurrence or nonoccurrence of a behavior immediately following a specified interval of time)

Step 2: Describe materials used in data collection: e.g. stopwatch, worksheets, etc. If you use a checklist or special forms, attach them to this form.

Sheet of paper, pencil, wall clock.

Step 3: Describe reliability measures (interobserver agreement). Attach instructions that are given to the independent observers.

Two or three observers tallying. See definition on page 000. Independent observers were instructed to tally in accordance with that definition. Previous reliability checks resulted in agreement ranging from 59% to 87%. Those checks brought about the definition on page 149. Subsequent checks ranged from 90% to 100%.

Step 4: Will you group your data (mean, mode, median) or make entirely separate graphs for each student (parent, teacher)?

Separate graph.

Step 5: Graph your data on the attached forms.

D. *Procedures*

Step 1: Indicate the procedures you will use to achieve the objectives stated under B.

a) What independent variable (treatment) will be used to produce behavior change; e.g. reinforcement, curriculum material changes, social models and imitation, etc.?

Cueing, social modeling, operant positive reinforcement

b) What are the contingency criteria for delivery of treatment; e.g. continuous, fixed time intervals, variable time intervals, fixed number (ratio) of responses, variable number (ratio) of responses?

Cueing—always at beginning of treatment time interval; intermittently thereafter.
Social modeling and reinforcement continuous at first; at variable ratio thereafter.

c) If you are using reinforcers or other consequences that must follow the behavior but which cannot be delivered immediately, how will you bridge this time delay?

d) If others are delivering treatment (e.g. parents or teachers) how will you know that it has been delivered?

Teachers will provide treatment.
Delivery occurs while observer is present and recording.

Describe the procedures you will follow: (Sources: 1, 2, 4, 6, 7, Parts II, III)

1. The student was referred by his teacher because of "talking out." Initial observation confirmed that the student was very responsive to adult and student attention. He also did enough covert mimicking of others to suggest susceptibility to social modeling.

2. The technique selected incorporated both. Following the baseline period, the teacher—

a) Cued the entire class: "Let's see how many can talk only after raising their hands and being called upon" or words to that effect.
b) Chose a conforming student and said, "Good ——, you raised your hand before speaking."
c) Immediately called upon the target student for the next class contribution (if quiet while holding up his hand) and reinforced him as in (b).
d) Began frequently calling on target student operantly and reinforced desired behavior. Intermittently recued class and modeled other students exhibiting the desired behavior.
e) Called on target student less frequently after two days, continued cueing and modeling.

3. The procedures were implemented during 9:30–9:40 A.M. each day that the observation was scheduled.

4. Reversal and reimplementation were carried out with replicating effects per the baseline and implementation procedures, respectively. Post-checks to follow.

E. *Applied Behavior Analysis* (Source: 7, Part I)

The Reversal Design

1. $Baseline_1$—Record of ongoing behavior prior to intervention (Step 3).
2. Intervention procedure—Introduction of Step 4.
3. $Baseline_2$—Withdraw intervention procedures and return to $Baseline_1$ conditions.
4. Intervention $procedure_2$—Reinstate the intervention procedures (same as intervention $procedure_1$).
5. Post-checks.

The Multiple Baseline Design

A multiple baseline analysis can be used when two or more similar behaviors are emitted by the same subject, when the same behavior occurs in different stimulus conditions, or when the same behavior occurs in more than one subject. When these conditions exist, contingencies may be applied to one behavior then the other, in one stimulus condition then the next, or with one subject then sequentially with other subjects. Functional relationships are established if changes in each behavior correspond to experimental manipulations.

a) Select the design you will follow in order to evaluate the effects of your instruction. Indicate the design you have chosen below:

Reversal Design

b) Define the criteria used for changing conditions (e.g. fixed time for each, criterion levels, "stability," etc.)

Baseline = 3 observations, Treatment I = 5 observations, Reversal = 3 observations. Treatment II = 5 observations contingent upon meeting criterion of less than or more than 50% of baseline frequencies (on the average).

c) Label and define, on the graph, each condition you implement. These labels and definitions should be concise, but complete enough that others would know your tactics without making reference to your text.

Graph is figure 5–20.

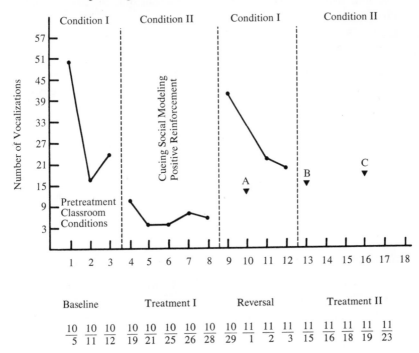

FIGURE 5–20

F. *Abstract*

Population and Setting:

1 12-year-old boy repeating 6th grade.
Self-contained class in a junior high school building.
Previous history of low achievement, misbehavior, reported "good" intelligence.

Target Behavior and Interobserver Agreement:

Vocalization (speaking out or making vocal noises in such a manner as to be disruptive) in the classroom. Interobserver agreements ranged from 90 to 100 percent.

Treatment and Result:

The teacher used verbal cueing (established a set), social modeling (positively reinforcing desired behavior emitted by another student) and operant positive reinforcement (when the target student responded in vocally appropriate ways) to reduce the vocalizations to less than 50% of baseline frequency.

Summary Statement:

The collected data were instrumental in demonstrating to the teacher her influence on the student's behavior. Upon seeing the data, the student agreed to work with the teacher in further lowering the number of his disruptive vocalizations.

References

Baer, D. M. and M. M. Wolf. "Recent Examples of Behavior Modification in Preschool Settings." In Newringer and Michael, eds., *Behavior Modification in Clinical Psychology*. New York: Appleton-Century-Crofts, 1970, pp. 10–25.

Baer, D. M., M. M. Wolf, and T. R. Risley. "Some Current Dimensions of Applied Behavior Analysis." *Journal of Applied Behavior Analysis* 1 (1968): 91–97.

Cooper, J. O., B. Jacobsen, and J. Payne. "A Program for Decelerating Multiple Mealtime Problem Behaviors of a Severely Retarded Preschool Child." Proceedings from *National Association for Retarded Children*

Conference on the Education of Mentally Retarded Persons, St. Louis, Missouri, September, 1971.

Foxx, R. M. and P. L. Martin. "A Useful Portable Timer." *Journal of Applied Behavior Analysis* 4 (1971): 60.

Journal of Applied Behavior Analysis. Society for the Experimental Analysis of Behavior, Inc., Lawrence, Kansas, 1968.

Lindsley, O. R. "A Reliable Wrist Counter for Recording Behavior Rates." *Journal of Applied Behavior Analysis* 1 (1968): 77–78.

Priser, J. "Project Breakthrough Report." Unpublished manuscript, Exceptional Children, Ohio State University, Columbus, Ohio, 1972.

Reynolds, N. J. and T. R. Risley. "The Role of Social and Material Reinforcers in Increasing Talking of a Disadvantaged Preschool Child." *Journal of Applied Behavior Analysis* 1 (1968): 253–62.

Risley, T. R. "Behavior Modification: An Experimental-Therapeutic Endeavor." Paper prepared for Banff International Conference on Behavior Modification, 1969.

Stanberry, M. and J. Harris. "Reduction of Tardy Behavior in Junior High School Pupils." In Hall, R. V., ed., *Managing Behavior Part 3.* H & H Enterprises, Inc., P. O. Box 3342, Lawrence, Kansas, 1971.

Wilson, G. "Project Breakthrough Report." Unpublished manuscript, Exceptional Children, Ohio State University, Columbus, Ohio, 1972.

Wolf, M. M. and T. R. Risley. "Reinforcement: Applied Research." Presented at the Annual Conference of the Learning Research and Development Center, University of Pittsburgh, 1969.

Appendix

Instrumentation for
Observational Recording

Instrumentation

The following instruments and techniques are useful for classroom teachers who wish to make observational recordings. Instrumentation for event, duration, interval, and time sample recording is presented.

Event Recording

1. *Wrist, golf-counters* are effective to tally student behaviors (Lindsley 1968). These counters can be purchased from sporting goods stores or large department stores. Most wrist counters will cumulate 0 to 99 responses per session. One disadvantage is that most are constructed to tally only one class of response. Wrist counters distributed by Behavior Research Company (see address and order number at end of paragraph) will accommodate two discrete behaviors. Counters from this company use two top windows to accumulate responses from 0 to 99 and a bottom window to count a second behavior up to nine occurrences

or to indicate hundreds if top counters go beyond 99. One approach to minimize the disadvantage of recording only one or two discrete responses is to use more than one counter. Two or three counters can be attached to the same wrist band. This tactic allows the directive teacher to record three to six different behaviors for one child, or one behavior for three to six children, or any combination of three to six discrete events or children. Wrist counters may be purchased from *Behavior Research Company,* Box 3351, Kansas City, Kansas 66103, order number 99 and 9wc, 0-99 and 0-9 wrist counter. Figure A-1 is a picture of a wrist counter.

*FIGURE A–1.　A Wrist Counter Sold by Behavior
Research Company*

2. *Hand Tally Digital Counters* follow the same recording principles as wrist counters. Hand tally counters are frequently used in food chain stores, cafeterias, or army mess halls to tally the number of people served. These counters may be constructed from metals or plastics. Metal counters appear to be more durable and are recommended, but the cost is higher than plastic models. Manual hand counters are avail-

able in single or multiple channels. Single-channel metal hand tally counters are available from Cambosco Scientific Company, Inc., 342 Western Avenue, Boston, Mass. 01235, order number 41-475. Five-channel manual counters are available from Lafayette Radio and Electronics, 111 Jerico Turnpike, Syosset, L. I., New York 11791, order "Multi Counter" #99C9031. The "Multi Counter" has dimensions of 5¼ by 1½ inches. The "Multi Counter" fits comfortably in the palm of the hand and, after some practice, can be operated rapidly and reliably using the fingers of the same hand. This counter has been operated more than 5000 times over a three-month period without evidence of malfunction (Mattos 1968). Figure A–2 contains pictorial examples of single- and multiple-channel manual counters.

FIGURE A–2. Single- and Multiple-Channel Manual Counters

3. *A Wrist Tally Board* is a note pad encompassed by plastic holder with a watch band. Teachers can conveniently use wrist tally boards for event recordings. Advantages include: (1) a convenience of having writing paper readily available, (2) multiple behaviors of a child or children can be recorded, and (3) notes and time can be recorded as well as numerical tallies. Wrist tally boards are sold by Behavior Research Company, Box 3351, Kansas City, Kansas 66103, order WTB, Wrist Tally Board, for note pad sets (12 pads with 30 cards each) order WRBPS. Dimensions of the wrist tally board are 3½ by 2¼ inches. Figure A–3 is an example of the wrist tally board.

4. *Noncommercial Tally Procedures:* Teachers have devised several excellent noncommercial tallying procedures. One procedure consists of cumulating frequency counts on masking tape attached to the wrist.

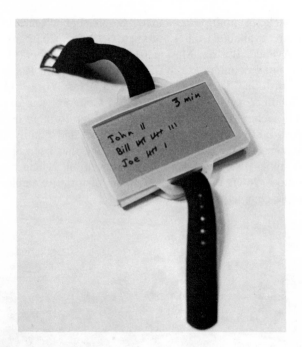

FIGURE A–3.   *Wrist Tally Board*

Another is to use buttons or paper clips to tally the number of times a behavior occurs. Initially, all buttons or paper clips are placed in one pocket. Immediately following the occurrence of a behavior to be recorded, the teacher places one paper clip or button in another pocket. A tally of the number of times an event occurs is then recorded at the end of the measurement period. A two-pocket apron is used when clothing does not have pockets. Each teacher who uses event recording can develop her own unique tally procedures.

Duration Recording

The most precise nonautomated instrument for duration recording is a *stopwatch*. There are two basic models. First, is a stopwatch for general timing which can be started, stopped, and returned to zero by successive depressions of the crown. See figure A–4. A disadvantage of this model is that it cannot accumulate durations of subsequent behavioral episodes. If this model is used to accumulate durations of subsequent behaviors, the previous duration must be recorded with pen and paper before starting another duration count.

   The second model contains a "time-out" feature which can be used to accumulate discrete episodes. These time-out instruments are started

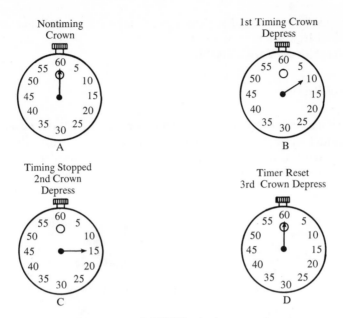

FIGURE A–4

and stopped by moving a side slide forward and backward or by successive depressions of the crown, depending on the type and make of watch. The hands are reset to zero by first stopping the timer by moving the side slide down, then depressing the crown; or with some models, by stopping the timer and depressing a side button. See figure A–5.

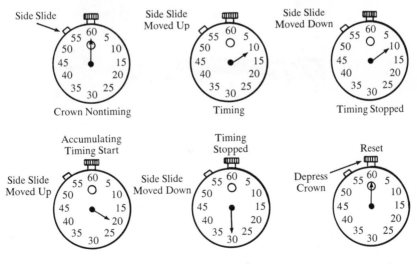

FIGURE A–5

For teachers interested in purchasing a stopwatch, a catalogue may be requested from Meylan Stopwatch Corporation, 264 West 40th Street, New York, New York   10018.

Interval Recording

A common timing device used in interval recording is *pen, paper, clipboard,* and stopwatch. The stopwatch should be attached to the clip of the clipboard. Commercial stopwatch attachment devices for clipboards are available, but the watch can be satisfactorily attached with rubber bands. Figure A–6 is a picture of a clipboard stopwatch timing device.

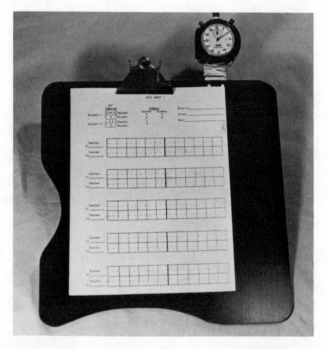

FIGURE A–6.   A Clipboard Stopwatch Timing Device

A disadvantage of using the clipboard-stopwatch timing device is that the observer must periodically break eye contact with his subject to observe the stopwatch.

Worthy (1968) described a miniature, portable timing and audible signal-generating device to be used as a time-base for interval recording. He reports that "this device, which is small enough to fit into a shirt pocket, eliminates the need for the observer to visually monitor a stopwatch, etc. which detracts from his observance and recording of behavior."

These devices are constructed so that programming can be set at different fixed intervals within a range of approximately three to twenty seconds. As the interval times-out, a signal with an audible beep is generated through the speaker or ear plug. An option includes a light signal without an audible stimulus. Following the signal, the timer recycles.

Concerning reliability of the timing units, Worthy reported:

> Three units were operating at the time of writing (with their original batteries), one of them with the Sonalert option. One of the speaker-type units has been operated for eight 12-minute sessions, daily, for the past three months. The other speaker unit and the Sonalert unit have about 30 and 48 hour respectively, of operating time spread over about 45 days. Tone interval repeatability, as measured with a stop watch, remains essentially constant.

> A fourth unit, assembled for testing purposes, was set for 10-second intervals, and operated continuously for 11 hours. At the end of that time, the battery was substantially discharged and output voltage was reduced to about half its original value, with a noticeable drop in the intensity of the tone, and a 10% deterioration in the timing interval. These preliminary findings indicate that the unit will generate highly reliable signals for many hours when used intermittently, but will show some deterioration in the reliability of the interval when exposed to sustained, continuous operation. (Worthy 1968)

Worthy's technical note is complete enough so that most TV-radio repairmen could build the timing device. Also, Scott Behavioral Electronics, Inc., Box 3306, Lawrence, Kansas 66044, sell audible recycling timers, the Scott Fixed 10 second pocket timer and variable time adjustment timers. Figure A–7 shows timers built from plans given in Worthy's (1968) technical note.

Time Sample

A teacher can use a *wall clock* or a *wrist watch* for time sampling. However, when giving instruction it is difficult to time intervals without a signal device.

Common *kitchen timers* have been found to be useful as a signal device for time sample measures. The Lux Minute Meter Timer is an inexpensive timing device with a one year guarantee against defects. The timer can be set at minute intervals up to one hour. Lux Minute Meter Timers are sold by Robertshaw Controls Company, Lux Time Division, Lebanon, Tennessee or Waterbury, Connecticut. Figure A-8 presents the Lux Timer.

FIGURE A–7.   *Timers Built from Worthy's Technical Note*

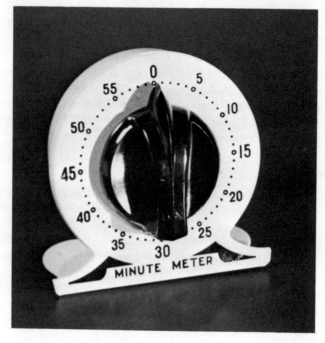

FIGURE A-8.   *Lux Minute Timer*

Foxx and Martin (1972) reported a technical note on a portable timer (Memo-Timer, manufactured in Switzerland) which can be set in five-minute intervals up to one hour. They report that the timer weighs "barely an ounce, . . . can be attached to a belt, worn inside a pocket, or pinned to the clothing." Furthermore, they state that the "timer was accurate to within one minute, suggesting that it is useful when a fine degree of accuracy is not required. Our experience with timers has been that they run faster than indicated and should always be tested to find the most reliable settings." Figure A-9 shows the Memo-Timer. The Memo-Timer may be ordered from Charles Alshuler Co., Box 3720, Milwaukee, Wisconsin   53217.

FIGURE A-9.   Memo Timer

References

Foxx, R. M. and P. L. Martin. "A Useful Portable Timer." *Journal of Applied Behavior Analysis* 4 (1971): 60.

Lindsley, O. R. "A Reliable Wrist Counter for Recording Behavior Rates." *Journal of Applied Behavior Analysis* 1 (1968): 77-78.

Mattos, R. I. "A Manual Counter for Recording Multiple Behavior." *Journal of Applied Behavior Analysis* 1 (1968): 130.

Worthy, R. C. "A Miniature, Portable Timer and Audible Signal-Generating Device." *Journal of Applied Behavior Analysis* 1 (1968): 159-60.

Glossary

Key words and phrases used in this book are defined below. The definition given is that used or implied in the book. For technical words and phrases used in this book but not included in the glossary or for more complete definitions see Owen R. White, *A Glossary of Behavioral Terminology*, Research Press, Champaign, Illinois, 1971.

A-B Design: A procedure for demonstrating amount of behavior change. This design cannot show what variables caused the behavior change. A-B Design—where behavior is measured (A) before (see baseline) and (B) during instruction.

Analysis: Identification of the effects of a teaching procedure on student behavior. Analysis is concerned with the amount of behavior in both the presence and absence of instruction. Instructional events are systematically manipulated to demonstrate that the teacher can exercise control over student behavior. The two designs most used in behavioral analysis are the *reversal* and *multiple baseline designs*.

Assessment: "A survey of student functioning to determine those responses and skills that are adequate and those yet to be learned or mastered" (Stephens 1970).

Baseline: The level or amount of behavior prior to the introduction of a teaching procedure. Baseline data are usually expressed in numerical terms of rate, frequency, percent, or duration. Teaching procedures are frequently introduced only after five or more sessions of baseline data have been collected.

Behavior: Refers to any act of an individual or group that is observable and measurable. Behavior can be external or internal. Used interchangeably with *response.*

Central Tendency: A statistic intended to typify measurement of group or individual behavior. Central tendency is a good approximation to a student's typical behavior. The *mean* and *median* are frequently used as an index of central tendency.

Continuous Recording: "This is sometimes called an anecdotal record. The observer attempts to write down everything as it happens" (Hall 1971).

Cumulative Graph: A graphic presentation of successive summed numbers (rate, frequency, percent, duration) representative of behavioral occurrences.

Data Point: A quantitative score of an individual or group behavior as reported on a graph.

Differential Reinforcement of Other Behavior: A procedure in which reinforcement is given contingent on the nonoccurrence of the target behavior.

Duration Recording: Recording the time that a behavior continues or lasts, usually reported as percentage of time.

Event Recording: A tally or frequency count of discrete events as they occur.

Frequency: The number of times a specific behavior occurs in a unit of time—a tally.

Functional Relationship: "A lawful relationship between two variables. In behavior modification, a dependent behavior and a given procedure are functionally related if the behavior systematically varies as a function of the application of the procedure" (Sulzer and Mayer 1972).

Interobserver Agreement Measures: Procedure to verify the reliability of the measurement of behavior. Reliability is usually concerned with the percentage of agreement among two or more independent observers on the occurrence or nonoccurrence of behavior. Percentage of interobserver agreement is calculated by dividing the number of agreements by the number of agreements plus disagreements and multiplying by 100.

Interval Recording: Used to measure the occurrence or nonoccurrence of a behavior within specific time intervals. Time intervals will usually range from six to thirty seconds depending on behavior to be observed. Behavior is usually recorded only once per interval and reported as percentage of occurrence.

Intervention: A systematic manipulation of teaching tactics.

Magnitude of Behavior Change: A quantity of behavior which is greater or less in some respect than prior behavior.

Mean: An arithmetic average of a set of data.

Median: The middle score in a ranked distribution.

Model: "That subject or device which demonstrates a performance or task to an organism in the operation of modeling" (White 1971).

Multiple Baseline: A multiple baseline analysis can be used when two or more similar behaviors are emitted by the same subject, when the same behavior occurs in different stimulus conditions, or when the same behavior occurs in more than one subject. When these conditions exist, contingencies may be applied to one behavior then the other, in one stimulus condition then the next, or with one subject then sequentially with other subjects. Functional relationships are established if changes in each behavior correspond to experimental manipulations.

Noncontingent Reinforcement: Consequences of behavior usually presented to the student on variable time or fixed time intervals regardless of student behaviors.

Noncumulative Graph: Sometimes called a line graph. Student scores are placed on squared graph paper. The amount of behavior (Y-axis) is plotted at the intersection of the time section (X-axis). After scores (data points) have been placed, they are connected by a line to form a polygon.

Observational Recording: When teachers or other individuals look at behavior and produce records of that behavior as it occurs.

Percentage: A ratio that reports data as a given amount in every hundred responses.

Permanent Products: Products that are tangible and can be measured any time after the students' behavior. *Written* spelling words, *written* arithmetic computation, and stringing beads are examples of permanent products.

Pinpointed Behavior: A specific, measurable behavior that is chosen for instruction.

Polar Behavior: Refers to opposite behavior sets such as in seat–out of seat, writing *was* for *saw,* talking–not talking.

Post-Checks: When a behavior is periodically measured after the teacher has formally terminated training for that particular behavior.

Range Scores: Difference between the lowest and highest score in a set of measurements.

Rate: Defined as the frequency of occurrence during a unit of time. Rate is calculated by dividing the frequency of occurrence by a unit of time (rate $= \dfrac{\text{frequency}}{\text{time}}$) and is usually expressed in responses per minute.

Reinforcement: Any consequence of behavior that increases the probability of occurrence of the behavior it follows.

Reliability: See *interobserver agreement measures.*

Reversal (ABAB) *Design:* A design for behavior analysis with four conditions: (A) Baseline$_1$, (B) Intervention$_1$, (A) Baseline$_2$, (B) Intervention$_2$.

Target Behavior: Same as pinpointed behavior.

Terminal Behavior: The criterion for student behavior.

Time Sampling: The measurement of the occurrence or nonoccurrence of a behavior immediately following a specified interval of time.

X-axis: With standard graphic arrangements, the X-axis is the horizontal axis and usually indicates units of time, e.g. minutes, sessions, days, weeks.

Y-axis: With standard graphic arrangements, the Y-axis is the vertical axis and usually indicates amount of behavior, e.g. frequency, rate, percent, proportion, duration.

Index